Progress in Geriatric Day Care

King Edward's Hospital Fund for London

King Edward's Hospital Fund for London is an independent foundation, established in 1897 and incorporated by Act of Parliament 1907, and is a registered charity. It seeks to encourage good practice and innovation in the management of health care by research, experiment and education, and by direct grants.

Appeals for these purposes continue to increase.

The Treasurer would welcome any new sources of money, in the form of donations, deeds of covenant or legacies, which would enable the Fund to augment its activities.

Requests for the annual report, which includes a financial statement and lists of all grants, and other information, should be addressed to the Secretary, King Edward's Hospital Fund for London, 14 Palace Court, London W2 4HT.

Progress in Geriatric Day Care

by

J C Brocklehurst
MD MSc FRCP (Glas and Ed)
Professor of Geriatric Medicine
University of Manchester

and

J S Tucker
BSc MB MRCP
Consultant Geriatrician
St Luke's Hospital Bradford

King Edward's Hospital Fund for London

British Library Cataloguing in Publication Data

Brocklehurst, John Charles
Progress in geriatric day care.
1. Aged—Great Britain—Care and hygiene
2. Community health services for the aged—Great Britain
I. Title II. Tucker, J S
III. King Edward's Hospital Fund for London
362.6'15 HV1481.G5

Progress geriatric
ISBN 1 85551 011 1

Produced and distributed for the King's Fund by
Pitman Medical Limited

Printed and bound in England by The Pitman Press, Bath

King's Fund Publishing Office, 126 Albert Street, London NW1 7NF

Preface

In undertaking the research reported in this book we have been greatly assisted by many people. King Edward's Hospital Fund for London provided the main financial support, and the Department of Health and Social Security also gave generous financial help.

Mrs Anita Watson BA carried out the field work in relation to patients, relatives, ambulance drivers and social services; Mrs Pauline Maher and Mrs Jean Picker contributed considerably to the analysis of the data and Mrs Diane Hennessey typed the manuscript. We gratefully acknowledge all their assistance and also that of our colleagues practising geriatric medicine (and their day hospital staff) who have provided our basic data by their careful answers to our somewhat complex questionnaires.

JCB and JST

Contents

Tables

1
Genesis and objectives

It often seems in Great Britain that our institutions, like Topsy, just grow. Ideas develop very often on the initiative of one or two people. Then money is found to try them out and the initiators by their enthusiasm infect other people, and so the new ideas are developed until a stage is reached when they seem to have passed into normal practice. On the face of it, this often seems a haphazard process and by the time the institution has been accepted as normal and national planning includes a provision for it, it may well be difficult to make a truly objective appraisal of its effectiveness. This progression of events has been the way in which many of the institutions involved in the care of old people have developed. Voluntary bodies have often been the first to experiment with new ideas; for instance, luncheon clubs, day centres, old people's residential homes of one type and another, sheltered housing, meals on wheels, good neighbour services, boarding out schemes and a host of others.

The geriatric day hospital developed from very modest beginnings 30 years ago with a number of old people attending hospital wards or occupational therapy departments after their discharge from the geriatric department; then one or two hospital chapels or ends of wards were adapted for this purpose. Since the first purpose-built day hospital was opened in Cowley Road Hospital in Oxford in 1958, development has been rapid so that day hospitals are now almost universal within departments of geriatric medicine. They are provided for in the planning of the Department of Health and Social Security, and indeed in a number of geriatric departments second and third day hospitals have been opened.

It is interesting to compare this development with that in other countries where the development of institutions depends, for one reason or another, on planning on a national scale. Perhaps the best example is the United States where it is now difficult for any operator (whether a charity, religious group or private entrepreneur) to provide a new institution for the care of old people drawing on some sort of financial support from the State until legislation has provided a formula by which such funds can be made available. This means that the move from experiments by voluntary bodies to the development of a State-funded (or partially State-funded) institution is marked by a clearly definable bridge. Before this bridge is crossed, it is likely that the State will require objective evidence to demonstrate beyond reasonable doubt that the institution will be effective for the purpose for which it is designed and perhaps indeed also be 'cost effective'.

There appear to be advantages in both systems. The British system may allow a more rapid development and response to new ideas, whereas the American may produce a better researched and possibly more effective institution, although after a gestation period which seems interminable both to the consumer and to the doctors and others.

Objectives

The purpose of the geriatric day hospital cannot be simply defined, as, for instance, can the family planning clinic, because it includes a number of objectives. These objectives apply to different patients at any one time and some of them may apply to any one patient at different times. The reason for a patient's attendance may change during the course of his treatment. Geriatricians regard rehabilitation, maintenance, assessment, medical, nursing and social care as the most important factors in the care of a day hospital patient. We now define these terms as we understand them.

Rehabilitation

The word is derived from the Latin *habilis* which means deft, and from this root come both 'ability' and 'rehabilitation'. Rehabilitation means to regain abilities, or to overcome disability, and comprises several elements—the recognition of disability and its cause, bringing about physical and psychological changes within the disabled person, and perhaps manipulating his physical and social environment. It is a process which anticipates recovery, or at least improvement, and is both dynamic and finite.

Maintenance

Maintenance logically follows rehabilitation and its objective is to maintain the degree of independence achieved by rehabilitation.

Assessment

Assessment is interpreted in different ways by different people—in a simplistic way it entails forming an opinion of the patient's physical, mental and social situation and devising a plan to achieve the optimum for that patient. The justification for regarding the day hospital as a suitable place for assessment is that here assessment is seen as a process requiring observations over a period, rather than at a single session.

Medical, nursing and social care

The need for medical supervision of patients, and for nursing care, requires no further explanation.

There are two main types of social reasons why patients may attend a day hospital. One is for the patient's direct benefit—to combat the effects of isolation; the second is for the benefit of his relatives or 'carers'—to relieve the strain of coping with a disabled, aged person, even sometimes to allow them to work when this would not otherwise be possible.

2

Design of the study

This book describes three surveys carried out in 1977 and 1978 in an attempt to portray the present range of geriatric day hospitals in Great Britain, to determine what is generally accepted as necessary in practice and to identify problems which still require solutions.*

The first survey was by a questionnaire sent to all 350 consultant geriatricians in Great Britain in 1977. Altogether, 226 questionnaires were returned completed and only nine of the respondents indicated that there was no day hospital in their units. In many cases more than one consultant worked in the day hospital but we asked that only one questionnaire should be returned for each day hospital. Information on 217 day hospitals was obtained.

Also, each area health authority was asked to indicate the number of geriatric day hospitals in the area and this yielded an overall figure of 302. The response rate to our questionnaire, therefore, in relation to the known number of day hospitals, was 72 per cent. It may even have been higher since some of the day hospitals included in the area health authorities' returns may have been for psychogeriatric patients, although respondents were requested to exclude this group.

*The full report of these surveys, including questionnaire forms, detailed analyses of data, architects' plans, may be seen in the library of the King's Fund Centre, 126 Albert Street, London NW1 7NF.

This questionnaire established general data about geriatric day hospitals in Britain; for example, where they were situated, whether or not they were purpose-built, the nature of transport to the hospital, average weekly attendances and of various grades of staff. From this it was possible to build up a picture of a representative British geriatric day hospital.

The second survey was by questionnaire to consultant geriatricians in 104 day hospitals in all parts of the country, which sought information, for one representative week in early November 1977, on the number of new patients who began attendance, the source of and reason for their referral, the number of patients discharged and the reason for their discharge. Information was also sought about the number and grade of all staff, the number of hours they spent in various activities and the types of technical procedures they carried out. From the information, it has been possible to build up a picture of the life of a geriatric day hospital.

The third survey aimed to discover in detail the general philosophy of the day hospitals, their methods of management, their design, the cost of running them, and the views of patients, their relatives, the staff and the ambulance drivers. Thirty day hospitals were visited, first by one of us (John Tucker) and later by a research assistant sociologist (Anita Watson).

The day hospitals were chosen to represent a wide cross-section of different geographical areas and different types of day hospital: five hospitals in Greater London; eleven in other industrial cities; nine in small towns; and five in rural areas (see Appendix).

The physicians were asked about the objectives of the day hospital and whether these were being fulfilled; also about the construction of the unit and its facilities, the management and operational policy of the unit, staffing problems and problems with transport. Of the 30 physicians interviewed, 21 were consultants, seven medical or clinical assistants and two senior registrars. At two day hospitals, a consultant and another doctor were interviewed, and at another two, no doctor was available for interview.

In 25 of the day hospitals, the nurses interviewed were sisters-in-charge; in the other five it was a registered or enrolled nurse. Nurses were asked about their perception of the aims of the day hospital and whether these were being fulfilled, the construction and facilities, the role of the nurse, teamwork in the day hospital, the kinds of patients being referred, nurses' involvement in teaching, and problems about nursing, staffing and transport.

Thirty physiotherapists and 24 occupational therapists were asked the same kinds of questions as the nurses and, specifically, about the facilities for rehabilitation and its practice.

Social workers were the most difficult to contact; many had too many other commitments to be available on the day of the visit. A social worker was interviewed at each of 14 day hospitals, and asked about her attitude to its policy, with questions similar to those addressed to the nurses, physiotherapists and occupational therapists. The social worker was also asked about links with local authority social services, with particular reference to day centres.

Other people interviewed were chiropodists, speech therapists, craft workers and dietitians.

The research assistant visited the day hospitals about two weeks after the physician, to discover the views of elderly patients and their relatives on the reasons why they used the day hospital, what they felt was most helpful and the problems they encountered. Interviews with patients were usually conducted in the day hospital, and the relatives were seen at home by appointment. The research assistant also interviewed ambulance drivers for their views about taking patients to the day hospital and on the suitability of their vehicles. The research assistant also surveyed the statutory day care provided for elderly people in the areas of these 30 day hospitals, by correspondence and occasionally by interviewing officials from the appropriate social services department.

3
Review of literature

Farndale (1961), whose book *The day hospital movement in Great Britain* describes the development of the concept of the day hospital, based his study on information collected from visits in 1958–9 to 38 psychiatric day hospitals, nine geriatric day hospitals and three day centres for the elderly.[26] Of geriatric day hospitals he wrote, 'Up to now day hospitals for old people are small and experimental. They operate on only a very limited scale.'

The idea of providing hospital facilities for patients without the 'hotel' services was first developed by psychiatrists. Arie (1975) wrote that day care was 'one of psychiatry's gifts to medicine'.[4] The first psychiatric day hospital was set up in Great Britain by Bierer in 1946 and the first geriatric day hospital at Cowley Road, Oxford, in the early 1950s. This unit was one of the nine visited by Farndale, who noted that the number of beds in the hospital had been reduced since the day hospital started, and the waiting list had disappeared. At the same time, Farndale felt that the day hospital for old people, unlike the psychiatric day hospital, was rarely an alternative to inpatient treatment but often to outpatient treatment or, very often, to attendance at a day centre or club. The emphasis in most day hospitals was said to be on occupational therapy.

Writing about his experience of the Cowley Road Day Hospital, Cosin (1954) contributed one of the earliest descriptions of a geriatric day hospital from the point of view of the physician.[17] He emphasised the importance of a thorough assessment of the patients attending and the need to design the treatment programme for each one. He suggested that patients made better progress if they were referred to the day hospital after, rather than before, admission to hospital. Another early description of a geriatric outpatient clinic with some of the features of a day hospital, which was formed in 1952, has been given by Droller (1958).[21] Other early descriptions include those of McComb and Powell-David (1961)[51], Fine (1964)[27] and Thomas and Williams (1966).[73]

Through the literature describing the first decade or so of geriatric day hospitals, the development of more rehabilitation can be traced. McComb and Powell-David described four categories of patients attending the day hospital which had been operating in Bolton for three years.

patients who were alone by day and needed care

patients who were lonely and had some physical or personality defect

patients requiring prolonged rehabilitation

patients who were pleasantly confused.

In 1969, Pathy also described four categories of patients attending the day hospital in Cardiff, his emphasis being rather different.

patients needing hospital services but not acutely ill and not requiring 24-hour nursing, especially if the disabling condition was predominantly physical, for example, arthroplasty, neurological disorders and limb amputations

patients requiring detailed investigation by special procedures patients discharged from hospital who required technical services and medical and nursing supervision for a while

inpatients who were ready to go home but worried about leaving hospital.

Pathy did not include confused old people in his four categories, and stated that in general they were best managed in a separate day unit. He quoted a mean attendance per patient at the psychogeriatric day hospital as 7.7 times that in the geriatric day hospital. He felt, however, that the same day hospital could cater both for patients primarily requiring medical supervision or nursing attention and those primarily requiring rehabilitation.[59]

The diagnostic and therapeutic function of the day hospital was emphasised by Andrews, Fairley and Hyland (1970) in their description of the day ward at West Middlesex Hospital, London. From 1962 to 1968 an average of about 80 new patients a year was seen and the average number of attendances was 13 (seven weeks). These authors stressed the importance of distinguishing between day hospitals and day centres.[3]

Brocklehurst (1973) suggested that it was particularly desirable to have the day hospital and geriatric rehabilitation unit sharing the same premises and facilities, and emphasised that patients should not be brought to day hospitals for procedures which could be carried out by the district nurse or the general practitioner in the patient's home.[11]

As the development of geriatric day hospitals escalated, the Department of Health and Social Security in 1971 issued guidelines for such units, proposing two geriatric day hospital places per 1000 elderly, and two psychogeriatric day hospital places per 1000 elderly, as a satisfactory provision.[31]

The Scottish Hospital Advisory Service (1973) convened a conference on a survey of eight day hospitals which suggested

> a major type for 30–50 patients, on the same site as a geriatric assessment unit
>
> an intermediate type for 15–30 patients, associated with long-stay beds, with more limited facilities but including rehabilitation
>
> a minor type for 10–15 patients, in semi-rural areas, associated with a limited number of long-stay beds.[32]

At the same conference the difficult questions of refusal and failure to attend were discussed: patients so confused that they might be further disoriented by the day hospital, patients too incapacitated to engage in any activities, patients unwilling to meet others and become part of the group. It was also noted that some patients referred to the day hospital could be adequately supervised at home by the general practitioners.

A symposium at Hastings in the same year was reported by Hall (1974).[36] There were contributions from representatives of all the disciplines concerned, and of the regional health authority and DHSS. Dr M K Thompson, a general practitioner, spoke of the lack of contact between the day hospital and general practitioners and said he had been the only one to visit the local day hospital for some years. He published a paper on this in 1974.[74]

Hildick-Smith (1977), in a survey of general practitioners in her area, found a good deal of confusion about the function of the day hospital but at the same time a desire to learn more.* General practitioners, however, are frequently employed part-time in day hospitals. Lloyd (1973) described the day hospital at Oldham, Lancashire, where five general practitioners were attached, one

*Hildick-Smith, M. *A study of day hospitals.* Unpublished thesis. Cambridge, 1977.

attending each day. Each doctor had patients allocated to him by the sister-in-charge after referral to the day hospital by one of the consultant geriatricians, thus each patient was seen by the same physician at each attendance. The general practitioners and the rest of the staff of the geriatric department held a lunch-time meeting every fortnight.[47]

Evaluation

For all the descriptions of day hospitals, there have been relatively few attempts to evaluate treatment. Woodford-Williams, McKeon and Trotter (1962) made the earliest outstanding contribution in their survey of former inpatients known to be living alone; 168 were attending a day hospital once a week (the treatment group) and 163 were not. Initially, attendance at the day hospital seemed to generate more admissions to hospital than non-attendance, but during the second six months of the survey period, the group attending the day hospital had fewer days as inpatients than the others. The benefit of close supervision at the day hospital was beginning to appear. Only 1 per cent of the treatment group went into local authority accommodation over the survey period compared with 4.9 per cent of the others. A detailed medical assessment was undertaken at the outset and repeated after 12 months. The results were scored, and there was some evidence of better scores in the treatment group, especially with regard to depression. Morale was said to be much better among the treatment group when they were admitted for inpatient treatment. They were anxious to get well, to return home quickly and to continue their attendance at the day hospital. The others made less effort to help themselves and resented the prospect of being discharged.[81]

Woodford-Williams and Alvarez continued their observations of the day hospital in their practice and in 1965 reported a study to determine the patients' needs, investigating the functions performed for each type of patient and exploring the possibility of reorganisation to increase efficiency. They studied a random sample of 100 of 260 current attenders and improvements were noted in 48. Significant numbers of patients attending for relief of strain on relatives or for physical and emotional dependence could equally well have attended a day club or workshop or, to relieve the relatives, a day ward—a ward in the geriatric department where the treatment would resemble that in an inpatient ward but with the patients going home at night. Such provision would be more appropriate for 'heavy' cases requiring constant supervision and for the mentally confused. It would be quieter than the day hospital and there would be less movement.[80]

Brocklehurst (1964) analysed the first 180 patients attending the Lennard Day Hospital, Bromley, and classified them according to age, source of referral, reason for attendance and diagnosis. The largest age group, 47 per cent, was 76–80 years. Fifty-three per cent of the patients were referred by general practitioners and 35 per cent were referred on discharge from the geriatric unit. Most of the patients (80 per cent) were attending for physical treatment and relatively few to avoid inpatient admission for social reasons (8 per cent). The commonest diagnosis was stroke. The outcome in these patients was examined, but the effect on inpatient beds was not determined. It was thought, however, that 11.8 per cent of patients had been able to go home earlier than would have been so otherwise. It was also thought that for 6.7 per cent admission to hospital was delayed and for 8 per cent prevented. Of particular interest was the observation that the group of patients aged over 85 was shown to have done just as well at the day hospital as the younger patients.[13]

In a further study of the same day hospital, Brocklehurst and Shergold (1969) reported a two-year follow-up of 200 patients discharged from two geriatric departments, only one of which had a day hospital, attended by 34 per cent of the discharged patients. The frailty of this group was emphasised by the fact that half of them had died, become ill at home or been readmitted to hospital within a year.[14]

Little information is available on the influence of age on physical rehabilitation, but Litman (1964) surveyed 100 disabled patients between 15 and 79 years and found that although the less responsive patients were on average slightly older than those who responded well, there was no general tendency for the older patients to lack desire for independence. He therefore found little evidence for an inverse relationship between age and response to rehabilitation.[46]

Brocklehurst (1970) evaluated the outcome for patients attending the Lennard Day Hospital over a six-year period, and attempted to determine the total provision of geriatric day hospitals in Great Britain at the end of 1969. The attitudes of geriatricians to day hospitals were explored, and it is noteworthy that only 4 per cent of the consultants questioned thought that day hospitals had little or no value.[12]

From a careful evaluation of the Royal Victoria Day Hospital, Edinburgh, Wadsworth, Sinclair and Wirz (1972) drew some interesting conclusions. Because some patients tend to become dependent upon the day hospital these authors thought that someone not in the day hospital's own team (perhaps a health visitor or social worker) should assume a 'dependency object' role and ease the patient's discharge. The division of responsibility between medical and social agencies made the transition from hospital to home more difficult and militated against optimal geriatric care in other respects. A common site for all forms of geriatric medical care, including the day hospital, was needed. Finally, there was an incompatibility between the stated objectives of the day hospital (particularly the saving of hospital beds) and life-supporting role for frail old people living at home.[76]

Tyndall and Ackroyd (1976) studied 660 referrals to Sherwood Day Hospital, Nottingham, over two years.* Its rehabilitative function was evaluated by observing changes in the degree of disability in patients during their treatment. Forty-five per cent of patients showed improvement, 40 per cent no change and 15 per cent deteriorated. Improvement in particular disabilities was as follows.

	% improvement
impaired mobility	52
disabling pain	49
incontinence	40
loss of dexterity	36
impaired speech	35
deafness	22
mental problems	22

An attempt to assess changes in personal independence, using subjective methods, showed only small numbers of patients restored to independence. The authors also attempted to determine prognostic indicators in day hospital patients. They found that age, sex and domestic circumstances did not differentiate patients, and that neurological conditions, dementias and, interestingly, skin conditions, carried a poor prognosis. A good prognosis was indicated by the absence of urinary incontinence.

Attempting to define patients' suitability for day hospital treatment (that is, patients actually attending and having planned discharges), the authors found that the 'successful' patients were younger and that rehabilitation had been the stated aim in over 90 per cent. The patients likely to have their attendance prevented

*Tyndall, R. *and* Ackroyd, H. *A survey of two years' work in the day hospital and a follow-up of patients referred.* Unpublished thesis, 1976.

or terminated for unexpected medical reasons had no special features except a higher incidence of genitourinary and rectal disease. Patients who were referred but refused to attend or who discharged themselves after a short time tended to be older and usually lived alone, and it was felt that the referral had often been more to ease the doctor's anxieties than to treat the patient. These patients came to no harm as a result of their refusal to attend the day hospital when compared with the 'successful' group.

Hildick-Smith (1977) discussed in some detail the difficulties in evaluation in a prospective survey of 1026 new patients attending the three day hospitals in East Kent between May 1971 and May 1972.* She found a higher proportion of long-term attenders (20 per cent) than Brocklehurst found in his Lennard Day Hospital survey (13 per cent) and felt that this reflected the almost total lack of day centres in the area.

Martin and Millard (1976) studied the workload of three day hospitals attached to departments of geriatric medicine over a year and found that the average length of a patient's attendance increased with the size of the day hospital from 5.5 weeks at the smallest (12 places) to 15.1 weeks at the largest (28 places). They also found that over two-thirds of patients achieved the objective of referral at the two smaller day hospitals, but less than one-fifth of patients did so at the 28-place one, despite the greater number of attendances and the longer periods of attendance. Since there were no significant differences in the illnesses of patients referred to the three day hospitals, it was suggested that the smaller ones could be more effective in rehabilitation, provided that they were principally staffed by remedial therapists. The larger day hospital had a higher proportion of nursing staff and was more custodial than rehabilitative. On the basis of this work, the authors described a new patient index (NPI) to indicate the activity of the day hospital and allow comparison with others, and with itself, at

*See footnote, page 12.

different times. The index was based on the assumption that 10 visits to a day hospital was the optimum. It was calculated as follows.

$$\text{NPI} = \frac{\text{Number of new patients} \times 10}{\text{Number of new places} \times \text{number of days worked}}$$

Martin and Millard suggested that the NPI gave a much more accurate assessment of the efficiency than did conventional returns of attendance, and that an NPI should be quoted in future papers attempting to evaluate day hospitals.[53]

Controlled comparisons are relatively rare. Washburn and Vannicelli (1976) made a controlled comparison of psychiatric day treatment and inpatient treatment, randomly assigning 59 psychiatric inpatients, all women, to day hospital care or continued inpatient care after two to six weeks. They found day treatment superior to inpatient with regard to subjective distress, functioning in the community, the burden to relatives and the number of days of attachment to the hospital programme. Interestingly, though, by 18 months to two years the advantages of attending the day hospital had largely disappeared.[77] The techniques of these authors are more applicable to psychiatric than to geriatric patients. The need for much more objective evaluation of the effect of day hospital treatment remains.

Day hospitals abroad

Much of the literature from the United States throughout the 1970s concerned descriptions of day care programmes, similar to that from Great Britain which appeared in the late 1950s and 1960s. Kostick (1974) has described a day care programme at the Levindale Hospital designed to serve old people with a lower functioning capacity than those attending 'senior centres'. The patients and staff of the hospital did not welcome the day patients, and a special area with day care staff was therefore created although the day patients continued to use the other facilities of the hospital. Social contact between day patients and inpatients, however, remained minimal.[45]

Gustafson (1974) described two day care centres in Honolulu. She also indicated that problems arise when the same administrators, nurses and social workers work in both the inpatient and the day care programmes. The point is also made that the British geriatric day hospital cannot be used as a model for the USA until geriatric medicine has developed. Gustafson suggested that private houses be used as neighbourhood day care centres for small numbers of patients, perhaps staffed by a married couple who own the house. This form of day care would be limited to well, ambulant clients, unless the staff were nurses. Such centres would be licensed in a way comparable to those undertaking the day care of children.[34]

Evaluations of geriatric day care in the United States have been published. Turbow (1975) has reviewed the progress of patients attending day care programmes.[75] Lorenze and others (1974) have described a project to determine whether the day hospital at the Burke Rehabilitation Center will prevent or postpone institutional care.[50] This day hospital was an adaptation of the British model to the American system. Kennedy (1975) has described a project to analyse the cost and determine the therapeutic impact, using experimental and control groups from the population referred to the day hospital.[42]

In describing a day care programme at a nursing home in Syracuse, New York, Mehta and Mack (1975) stressed that the referring physician, who may not be involved in the day hospital work, should remain in clinical charge of the patient. The physician received a letter each month after the multidisciplinary meeting in the day hospital.[55] Koff (1974) described a day care programme in a Jewish nursing home where day patients had the same range of services as residents, and two beds were kept for their use when necessary.[44]

There is now much interest in the USA in day care as an alternative to institutional care. The latter is a commoner solution to the problems of the disabled elderly in the USA.

Rathbone-McCuan and Levenson (1975) suggested much ambiguity about the structure and function of geriatric day centres in the United States.[63] In an attempt to resolve this, Robins (1975) proposed four different modules which would allow decisions to be made about types of day care which might qualify for national funding, and which in turn would set the pattern for day care in the future.* Module 1 provides full medical and rehabilitative services as an alternative to inpatient care. Module 2 provides rehabilitation after discharge from hospital, medical supervision being provided by the patient's personal physician. Module 3 provides 'long-term health maintenance to a high-risk population'—those approaching the need for long-term inpatient care—and the consequent relief for the relatives. Module 4 provides 'preventative care for all frail elderly who primarily require psychosocial activities in a protected environment'. Robins indicated that experimental programmes for modules 2 and 3 had been set up by the Department of Health, Education and Welfare by 1975.

Weissert (1976) studied 10 American day care programmes for adults and found they differed in virtually every important respect: history, affiliation, criteria and procedures for admission, characteristics of patients, staffing patterns, services given, facilities, costs and sources of support. He described two broad groups of day care: the physical rehabilitation programme called 'adult day care' which includes containment of disabled people,

*Robins, E.G. *Operational research in geriatric day care in the United States.* Paper presented at the 10th International Congress on Gerontology, Jerusalem, 1975.

many of them in wheelchairs and under 65 years; and a mixture of social rehabilitation to alleviate social isolation, improve nutrition and provide recreation. The participants in the latter type tend to be somewhat older and the cost is generally less.[79]

Among papers read at a conference on day care for older adults at the Center for the Study of Aging and Human Development, Duke University, in 1977, was *Physical health models of day care* by Charlotte Hammil, a detailed description of an experimental day hospital set up in 1972 under a grant from the US Department of Health, Education and Welfare in association with the Burke Rehabilitation Center.* The average daily attendance was 54, and 33 per cent of the patients were under 60 years of age. Stroke, arteriosclerosis and neurological disorders, such as disseminated sclerosis and Parkinsonism, predominated. The facilities included medical supervision, nursing, physiotherapy and occupational therapy, speech therapy and social work. This day hospital has many similarities to the British system, including similar problems. Hammil said 'managing transportation presents the greatest challenge, the greatest amount of frustration and the greatest single expense'. The day care service also included 'community out-reach'—a form of community screening service. Sources of reimbursement when the unit became self-supporting were 60 per cent from Medicare, 23 per cent from Medicaid, 12 per cent from major medical insurance and 2 per cent direct payment from the client.

Many attempts at evaluating day care programmes in North America have a distinctly sociological flavour. Some have been described above. Others include the work of Rathbone-McCuan and Levenson (1975), who considered the adequacy of 'social role performance' in day patients and inpatients at the Levindale Geriatric Research Center and described the introduction of a 'socialization therapist' to develop group therapy.[63]

*In a conference report, *Day care for older adults*, from the Center for the Study of Aging and Human Development, Duke University, North Carolina, 1977.

Weiler and Kim (1976) described a study to analyse the cost-effectiveness of a day care programme for the elderly, comparing an experimental group of participants in day care with a control group of elderly in the community. The physical and emotional functioning, activities of daily living, degree of institutionalisation, interpersonal relationships and the re-establishment of life style were evaluated in both groups. The experimental group showed improvement and differed significantly from the control group in emotional functioning, self-maintenance and relationships.[78]

Flathman and Larsen (1976) evaluated three geriatric day hospitals in Alberta and found great variations between the three but in general the patients thought to be suitable for day hospital treatment were those with physical problems (strokes, arthritis, fractures) and psychosocial problems (depression, family problems, social isolation, lack of motivation), and those whose families needed relief. Patients thought to be unsuitable included those with serious psychiatric problems, Parkinson's disease, multiple sclerosis, severe disability and those with long-standing problems. Patients in nursing homes were thought to be unsuitable. The patients' views were canvassed about day care. Six per cent would have preferred inpatient treatment and 12 per cent treatment at home by day hospital staff. This was partly because of transport problems. Follow-up of 66 patients showed some improvement in general health, independence and life satisfaction. Recommendations included placing geriatric day hospitals close to the various other facilities for care so that help could be given efficiently and economically, and medical and other agencies could be better informed about day hospitals. The authors concluded that the prime object of the day hospital should be the development and maintenance of patients' independence with frequent reassessment of their progress, and that public transport should be used whenever practicable. They also thought that social care should be developed independently of day hospitals.*

*Flathman, D.P. *and* Larsen, D.E. *Evaluation of three geriatric day hospitals in Alberta.* Medical Services Research Foundation of Alberta, and Alberta Hospital Services Commission, 1976.

It will be apparent from the North American studies that the clear distinction between day hospitals and social day centres, insisted on by most workers in Great Britain, does not apply to the same extent.

Descriptions of day hospitals and their patients in other countries have also been published. Blake (1968) described the first year of the John Lindell Day Hospital, Bendigo, Victoria, Australia, and made the interesting comment that the commonest primary diagnosis was 'senility'—that is, no gross pathological lesions but a severe degree of infirmity due to age.[9]

Hagvall and Suurkala (1975) have described three years' experience of their day hospital in Gothenberg, Sweden.[35] Dinse and others (1975) have outlined the planning for the Berlin–Charlottenburg Day Hospital.[19] Robins (1975) described two geriatric day hospitals in Israel, where high priority was being given to the development of home health services and day hospitals for the elderly. The two day hospitals—Shaarej Zedek, Jerusalem, and Tel Hashomer, Tel Aviv—were on the British model.[64] Löbl (1977) described day hospitals in Scandinavia.[48]

Staff

Among descriptions of the role of workers in the day hospital, Strouthidis (1974) outlined medical requirements[71], Saunders (1974) described the role of nurses[67], and Fairclough (1976), writing about a psychiatric day hospital, emphasised the nursing role.[25] There are, however, few descriptions of nurses or of remedial therapists.

Brocklehurst (1970) showed that, in 49 of 90 day hospitals he studied, the person regarded as being in overall charge was a nurse, compared with 16 where it was an occupational therapist, and even smaller numbers where it was someone from another profession. He reported that less than one-third of the geriatricians regarded nursing procedures as important aspects of day care, although bathing was provided at 80 of the day hospitals and enemata at 70.

His detailed study of five of the 90 day hospitals included analysis of sessions per week (session = 3½ hours). The mean total for remedial therapists and aides was 52, for nurses (all grades) 40 and for medical staff 10.[12]

Irvine (1969) emphasised the importance of encouraging the patients' relatives to visit the day hospital and learn some of the simple techniques of remedial therapy.[40] Ransome (1974)[62] and Marston (1976)[52] have described the work of physiotherapists. Discussion of the role of the occupational therapist in the day hospital has appeared more frequently in American literature; for example, Kiernat (1976)[43] and Aronson (1976).[5] The role of the occupational therapist in social services, including work with patients at home, and the organisation and supervision of craft work and activity groups in day centres, has been described by Higgins (1974).[37]

Bagnall (1974) discussed the social worker's place in the day hospital.[6] Eastman (1977) argued that social workers should 'throw off the yoke' of medical diagnosis when dealing with confused elderly patients because many of the symptoms of 'dementia' may have roots in social causes, and that treating the confused elderly as a group can lead to stereotypes and pessimistic views of containment and institutionalisation.[22]

The British Medical Association's report (1976) quoted the numbers of staff for geriatric day hospitals recommended by the South East Metropolitan Regional Hospital Board in 1970. These were, for 30 day hospital places: two physiotherapists, two occupational therapists and four physiotherapy/occupational therapy aides. The BMA working party regarded these numbers as reasonable, but commented that they were unlikely to be achieved for some time because of staff shortages.[10]

Recommendations for staffing a day hospital were made by the Wessex Regional Hospital Board (1972).* The recommended one nurse for six day hospital places is much more generous than the funded establishment of most geriatric day hospitals. A more usual ratio would be one nurse for 10–12 places. No recommendations were made on nursing grades, but a 1:1 ratio of qualified to unqualified staff is usual. The Wessex RHB's recommendations for remedial therapists were two physiotherapists and two occupational therapists (maximum of three of each) and four aides for 30 places. Most remedial therapists working in day hospitals also treat inpatients. If the day hospital is used for inpatient rehabilitation, more staff would be needed there. The Wessex recommendation for social workers was one per 50 places.

Day centres

The role of social services in providing day care was discussed at a conference at Hastings in 1973. Symonds (1974) thought that day care must include opportunity for recreation and real enjoyment.[72] Workshops for the elderly, of which there were more than 100 in Great Britain at the time, should be run like small businesses with work which offered some variety, avoided monotony and allowed conversation (Glass, 1974).[28] Matthews (1974) regarded residential care as a more pressing need than day care, and thought that putting day centres in the grounds of old people's homes for economic reasons might be detrimental to both residents and day clients.[54]

*Wessex RHB was incorporated in Wessex Regional Health Authority in 1974 during the reorganisation of the British National Health Service. The report may be obtained from Wessex RHA or the King's Fund Centre Library, 126 Albert Street, London NW1 7NF.

Anderson (1972), reporting the whole range of day care and leisure facilities for the elderly, described those in Teesside as an example: 'clubs and social centres exist for all old people to increase social contact and to give scope and facilities for new pursuits in retirement'. Day care centres should be able to provide a substantial amount of personal care to at least a few of the clients and there should be rehabilitative as well as recreational facilities. Such centres should be open seven days a week, with transport available. Psychogeriatric day care centres would be more supervisory though the same ancillary services and a substantial amount of occupational therapy would be provided. Day care in residential homes usually involved only a small number of clients; alternatively, a social club from the home might be of more benefit both for the residents and those who visit. Social centres or clubs vary in facilities and can often be successfully organised by retired people themselves. Anderson described rest centres, lunch clubs and work centres and the use of communal rooms in sheltered housing and other housing schemes.[2]

Another important survey of day care was that by Morley (1974), who examined facilities and services, staff training and the role of voluntary organisations.[56]

A survey of clients attending day centres and luncheon clubs over a two-week period was reported by the South Glamorgan County chief executive (1977).* Almost half the clients interviewed were aged over 75. Potential spare capacity was identified in four day centres and six luncheon clubs, the attendance being quite variable. Most clients came for meals and friendship: 66 per cent belonged to no other organisation, 66 per cent lived alone, 20 per cent relied on relatives or others for shopping and 15 per cent either had no hot meals except at the centre or only managed to cook

Survey report.** ***Provision of day centres for the elderly, **by the chief executive, South Glamorgan County, 1977.**

with difficulty. Most of the clients made their own way to the day centres: 60 per cent on foot and 10 per cent by bus; 22 per cent came by social services transport.

Most day care is provided in premises which may be used for other purposes. Robinson (1977) described a centre at Bridgnorth which used premises for adult education as 'a case of modest success', and suggests similar combined use of premises in areas with poor facilities.[65] An interesting alternative is the mobile day centre in Sunderland (Kaim-Caudle 1977) which was provided by Help the Aged, managed by Age Concern and run by the social services department. It is used three days a week at different sites, from 10am to 3pm, providing meals, company and simple activities for up to 14 people. The cost, in 1976, was less than £2 per user per day.[41]

Lodge and Parker (1977) discussed the importance of the environment and attitudes in day care, especially in encouraging individuality with a balanced programme to meet the needs of each client.[49]

The amount of assessment carried out in day centres is variable. Eastman (1976) described a day centre run by the London Borough of Newham social services department's day care division which placed emphasis on assessment: medical assessment was done by a community physician on the staff, educational assessment by an adviser from the education department, activities of daily living by an occupational therapist on the staff, and cognitive and psychological assessment by a community psychologist. Speech therapy and chiropody were also available. Clients were referred from various agencies, mainly from social workers and advisers to the disabled (occupational therapists), and assessment was reviewed monthly at a case conference. After three months a further review was made to decide if the client could be discharged or needed more time at the day centre to complete the assessment programme or to continue care. Clients who had reached maximum potential but needed continuing care could be transferred to a 'containment section' in the same building or to the luncheon club in the annexe to the day centre.[23]

The Newham day centre has many similarities to a day hospital and raises the question of the extent to which day centres and day hospitals should work together. This question has been discussed by Silver (1970)[69] and Williams (1975 and 1976)*, and we shall come back to it later in relation to our own findings.

A cost-benefit analysis of day centres in Leicester was undertaken by P A Management Consultants Ltd (1972). This indicated that savings would not cover annual operating costs, and that, for an economic return of 8 per cent, at least 70 per cent of attendances at a day centre would have to be by people who would otherwise have to be admitted to residential care and/or people whose relatives would be freed for paid employment. It was suggested that more use of day care in residential homes might be more economic.†

Transport

Many reports on day hospitals, in Great Britain and elsewhere, refer to transport as one of the greatest problems. It can be both a constraint on the effective use of professional staff in the day hospital and a source of anxiety, or even hazard, to the patients. The vehicles may not be available for day hospital patients because they are being used for accidents and emergency admissions. Vehicles used for these purposes are unsuitable for day patients;

*Williams, T.C.P. *Old for new.* Paper read at 10th International Congress on Gerontology, Jerusalem, 1975. *And, Joint venture in day care between hospital and local authority.* Paper read at a meeting of the British Geriatrics Soceity, Royal College of Physicians, London, autumn, 1976.

†*Cost benefit analysis in social services for the City of Leicester.* A report by P A Management Consultants Ltd to the Social Service Department, City of Leicester, 1972.

minibuses are much better (Brocklehurst 1970[12], Hildick-Smith 1974[38]). Hildick-Smith described a 21-mile round trip to the Dover day hospital, taking 1½ hours to collect eight patients.[38]

In a study of outpatients attending a physiotherapy department, Beer and others (1974) found that about 12 per cent were being brought by ambulance, and the average travel and waiting time amounted to 2½ hours. The authors stated that important side effects of outpatient treatment were fatigue and anxiety generated by ambulance transport.[8]

Howat and Kontny (1977) studied 1600 attendances at a psychiatric day hospital by 412 patients over one week. Thirty-three per cent came by ambulance; of these, 71 per cent were aged 65 and over, and 77 per cent could have travelled by car or taxi at less cost.[39]

The National Corporation for the Care of Old People (NCCOP) published proceedings of a conference on outpatient ambulance transport (1978).[57] Peak times of demand–early morning and late afternoon–for outpatient clinics, day hospitals, physical medicine departments, five-day wards, inpatient admissions and discharges, coincided with the peak times for accident and emergency cases.

Improvements might come if transport were provided only for strictly medical reasons, if advance notice could be given for routine ambulance requirements, if clinic and day hospital times were staggered and if the hospitals appointed someone to co-ordinate ambulance services.

A survey of transport to 16 day hospitals was reported at the NCCOP conference. Arrival time at the day hospital for the first patients was 8.30–10.00am (mean 9.20am) and for the last patients 10.20–11.45am (mean 11.00am). Departure time for the first patients was 3.00–3.45pm (mean 3.30pm) and for the last patients 4.00–5.00pm, though sometimes this could extend to 7.00pm. Journeys varied between two and 16 miles (mean 10 miles). One question arising from this survey was: should patients who could get themselves into ambulances without assistance be attending a day hospital?

Costs

Several authors have referred to cost as part of their descriptions of day hospitals, and we have mentioned some of these above. Farndale (1961) found only one geriatric day hospital which was costed separately in his survey, for which the total annual running cost was £6000, and the cost per patient per day worked out at 26/– (£1.30). Added to this was the cost of ambulance transport which worked out at 9/– (45p) per patient per day. Farndale felt that, in general, day hospitals might not necessarily be cheaper than inpatient treatment, but made the point that it might not be valid to compare the two, the maintenance of independence of patients in the community being an acceptable aim whatever the cost. Day hospitals were not saving any money, he reasoned, because beds were still full and there was usually a waiting list, but the day hospital might be the most economical way of spreading the facilities round a greater number of patients.[26]

Woodford-Williams, McKeon and Trotter (1962) discussed the cost of the Sunderland day hospital as part of an evaluation of that unit, quoting the cost per patient per day as 14/8½d (73p approximately) compared with the cost of inpatient treatment as 92/– (£4.60) per week.[81] Several North American authors have also compared the cost of day care with institutional care (Weiler and Kim 1976).[78] At the conference of the Scottish Hospital Advisory Service in 1973 it was said that accurate data on the cost of day hospital care were not available, but that it was estimated to be about one-third of the cost of inpatient treatment.[32]

Also in Scotland, Ross (1976) computed the cost for a patient attending a 30-place day hospital in Glasgow as £4, plus £2 for ambulance transport, per attendance. This is compared with a daily cost in a local authority residential home of £4, in a geriatric hospital of £7, and in a teaching hospital of £20. He noted, though, that the cost of running a local authority home, and perhaps of receiving other support in the community, must be added to the cost of day hospital attendance, and concluded that if patients are living alone it may be cheaper (though not necessarily better) for them to go into a local authority home.[66] Similar conclusions were drawn by Opit (1977), who studied the cost of domiciliary care for the elderly sick in 139 patients under the care of the home nursing service. His detailed breakdown of costs included nursing, social services (home helps, meals on wheels, chiropody), laundry services, day hospital attendance, indirect costs such as the cost of living at home with help from neighbours and members of the family. The range of direct costs varied from £2.95 to £83.75 per week with a mean of £25.60. Adding an indirect factor of £15, the argument was advanced that for some 20 per cent of the sample studied, home care was more expensive than a geriatric hospital.[58]

McFarlane and others, studying costs of the Victoria Geriatric Day Hospital, Glasgow, quote £13.70 per patient per day, which includes ambulance costs, but state that to this should be added the cost of community support for the patient at home, which is estimated at £13 per week.*

A detailed discussion of the use of cost-effectiveness analysis in geriatric day care has been given by Doherty and Hicks (1975). They suggest identification of the cost of three types of care for day patients.

*Personal communication from R McFarlane. The study was being undertaken at the same time as our own (JCB and JST).

primary services–all medical and other services provided in the day hospital

secondary services–services needed other than in the day hospital which may include medical, nursing, home help and other services

tertiary services–expenses normally incurred in living at home.

The authors discussed the difficulties of introducing objective cost-effectiveness analysis and concluded that, until such a method is developed, evaluation of day care will probably continue to rely on multiple, relatively independent indices of effectiveness. They suggested standardisation to obtain realistic measures.

uniform definition of cost, using appropriate costing models

agreement on cost-accounting procedures

a set group of output and outcome measures

use of similar timing for collecting data on outcome

definition and recognition of the role of services and patient/days as the final output of the system, but as intermediate output in the 'production' of the patient's welfare.[20]

4

A representative geriatric day hospital

Summary

A representative day hospital is described, embodying information supplied by questionnaire to 217 geriatric day hospitals.

Seventy-one per cent of the day hospitals were opened in the 1970s: 50 per cent are purpose-built. In 67 per cent there are separate physiotherapy and occupational therapy departments in the day hospital, and 71 per cent serve as a rehabilitation base for some of the geriatric inpatients. In 36 per cent special provision is made for psychogeriatric patients.

Day hospitals are generally well staffed. Thirty-four per cent of the consultants answering our questionnaire worked in more than one day hospital, and 54 per cent of day hospitals have more than one consultant. Consultants are clinically involved in 70 per cent of day hospitals and clinical assistants in 13 per cent.

State registered nurses are on the staff of 84 per cent of the day hospitals, State enrolled nurses in 71 per cent and nursing auxiliaries in 82 per cent. Physiotherapists work in 86 per cent of the hospitals but almost two-thirds of these have only the equivalent of one whole-time physiotherapist. Occupational therapists work in 68 per cent of day hospitals, but 57 per cent of these have only the equivalent of one whole-time occupational therapist. Therapy aides work in about two-thirds of day hospitals. Social workers are available for about three-quarters of day hospitals and speech therapists for about two-thirds. Most day hospitals (84 per cent) have some regular secretarial or clerical help.

Our representative geriatric day hospital opened in 1972 in a geriatric hospital (not a general hospital). It is purpose-built, and has its own occupational therapy and physiotherapy departments. It is used for treating day patients and inpatients requiring rehabilitation, but psychogeriatric patients are not accepted.

Two consultants work together and there are clinical assistants, nurses, physiotherapists, occupational therapists and aides on the staff. Social workers and a chiropodist are available.

Patients are accepted up to five days a week and there is no lower age limit. The catchment area is a defined one with a population of between 21000 and 30000 people aged 65 and over. The average number of patients attending weekly is between 51 and 100 and the average daily attendance is between 10 and 20. They are brought in by ambulance. The number of new patients admitted in 1976 was between 151 and 200. There is a social day centre in the locality to which patients are occasionally transferred.

This profile is subject to wide variation, however, as the findings from the postal questionnaire will show. Of the 226 questionnaires returned completed, nine were from respondents with no day hospital, and we have therefore used only the information from 217 geriatric day hospitals.

It is not easy to compute exactly how many day hospitals there are in Britain. The term is variously used and covers a number of very small establishments run as day wards rather than day hospitals and perhaps not even officially recognised. Enquiry of all area health authorities in 1977 suggested a total number of 302, and this is likely to be the maximum since a number of psychogeriatric day hospitals may also have been included in this figure. Altogether, therefore, information has been obtained for approximately 72 per cent of the day hospitals in Great Britain, although in some cases the answers provided in the questionnaires were incomplete.

One-third of consultant geriatricians work in more than one day hospital (34 per cent of 188 consultants answering this question). Geriatric departments generally have beds in more than one hospital. Indeed, all medical planning over the last few years has emphasised the need for some geriatric beds to be in a district general hospital, implying that others may be elsewhere; for example, in a 'community' hospital. Consequently, geriatric day hospitals may be developed in more than one hospital. Just over half the day hospitals (54 per cent) are staffed by more than one consultant. Of these, 36 per cent have two consultants; 12 per cent have three; 6 per cent have more than three. Two day hospitals have five and one has seven.

Seventy-one per cent of day hospitals were opened in the 1970s (figures derived from 210 replies). The time spread is as follows.

	%
1953–9	1
1960–9	28
1970–4	41
1975–7	30

This indicates that the momentum of development has continued at the same high rate since 1971. The figures show that 61 day hospitals were open in 1969 and a further 149 since then. The former figure does not coincide with that of a previous survey (Brocklehurst 1970) which showed a total of 90 day hospitals opened by 1969.[12] Allowing for some imprecision in answers to this question, it nevertheless seems likely that some day hospitals opened since 1969 have replaced others. Exactly half the day hospitals have been purpose-built.

Thirty-four per cent of the day hospitals were situated within a district general hospital. This shows a change from the 1970 survey in which 46 per cent of the day hospitals then existing were in general hospitals, and suggests that the more recent emphasis has been on building day hospitals away from the district general hospital site. No doubt this is partly accounted for by the development of a second or third day hospital for one geriatric service. Fifty-one per cent are now in geriatric hospitals, 4 per cent are on sites separate from any hospital, and the remaining 11 per cent are in a variety of sites, including mental hospitals, general practitioner hospitals, a converted children's hospital and so on. Perhaps most of these would now be described as 'community' hospitals.

Two-thirds of day hospitals (67 per cent) have separate physiotherapy and occupational therapy departments in the day hospital itself. In the remainder the day hospital does not contain these departments: they are in another part of the hospital (in 28 per cent) or in an outpatient department (in 5 per cent). In about one-third of these the department, whilst separate, is very close to the day hospital. In a few, the occupational therapy department is in the day hospital but physiotherapy is elsewhere. In 1 per cent there is no occupational therapy or physiotherapy department available to day hospital patients.

In 71 per cent of day hospitals in district general hospitals, the day hospital serves also as a rehabilitation base for some of the geriatric inpatients. This is a slightly lower percentage than in

1970 when 87 per cent shared with inpatients. It makes good sense for inpatients undergoing rehabilitation to use the day hospital—not only economic sense but also to allow patients, before they leave hospital, to become familiar with the day hospital and so feel more secure about their discharge because they know that contact with the day hospital will be continued thereafter.

Transport is provided by only the ambulance service in 61 per cent of day hospitals but additional or alternative arrangements are available in the remainder. This includes 10 per cent which have special transport for the day hospital and 29 per cent which use voluntary transport.

Whilst nearly all day hospitals (94 per cent of 208 replies) have a defined catchment area, and 65 per cent serve a population of 21000 to 30000 aged 65 and over, there is considerable variation. Fifteen per cent serve an estimated population of less than 20000 elderly and 20 per cent have catchment populations in excess of 40000. If the provision of day hospital places is based on the DHSS norm of two per 1000 aged 65 and over (DHSS 1971[31]), 15 per cent of day hospitals might be expected have 20 or fewer places and 20 per cent to have 80 or more.

Information was not obtained on the number of places available in each of the day hospitals, but it may be deduced from the number of attendances per week and the total number of new patients attending during 1976. Table 1 shows that most day hospitals have fewer than 100 patients attending each week while 17 per cent have more than 150. However, the daily attendance per patient cannot be deduced from these figures. This information is not available from the first questionnaire, but our survey of patients carried out in the third part of our study showed an average of 1.9 attendances weekly. Assuming an average of two days' attendance a week, most day hospitals would require fewer than 40 places.

Table 1 Average weekly attendance, and total new patients in 1976

*Average weekly attendance**	%	*Total new patients in 1976†*	%
1 - 50	16	51 - 100	23
51 - 100	46	101 - 150	24
101 - 150	21	151 - 200	16
151 - 200	10	201+	37
201+	7		

*203 replies

†141 replies (does not include day hospitals opened in 1976–7)

Note: 5 per cent of the day hospitals had more than 400 new patients in 1976.

Eighty-three per cent accept patients five days a week (based on 196 replies). Three day hospitals accept patients six days a week. Seven per cent accept patients only on one or two days a week and a further 10 per cent only three or four days.

About half the day hospitals (52 per cent) have no lower age limit. Some consultants indicated, however, that while they had an age limit, they sometimes accepted patients below it, particularly those with stroke illness.

Of the hospitals which have a lower age limit, it is 65 years in 69 per cent, between 50 and 60 years in 20 per cent, and the age of retirement (women at 60, men at 65) in 11 per cent.

Questions were asked about the provision of psychogeriatric day hospitals and about social day centres. Thirty-six per cent of day hospitals are in areas which have a separate day hospital for psychogeriatric patients (based on 166 replies); in 19 per cent, psychogeriatric patients share the geriatric day hospital and in 45 per cent there is no day hospital for psychogeriatric patients. The number with a separate psychogeriatric day hospital seems high (a total of 59), and this may be compared with the number of specialist psychogeriatricians appointed in the United Kingdom by 1977, which was about 50. It is clear, however, that only a few geriatricians see the day hospital as having both a geriatric and a psychogeriatric function. This is in line with the finding that only 21 per cent of consultant geriatricians in 1970 regarded social care of mentally confused as an important aspect of the day hospital service while 35 per cent saw it as being of little or no importance (Brocklehurst 1970).[12] At that time it was indicated that, despite these views, many patients attending were confused. (The extent to which mental confusion appears as a reason for day hospital attendance at the present time is discussed in Chapter 8.) But it is important to define the term 'psychogeriatric'. In the minds of most geriatricians it refers to patients who are attending specifically for the containment and management of chronic brain syndrome, whereas those with brain failure, in addition to other problems, may be seen as attending the day hospital for those other problems and therefore do not fall within the category 'psychogeriatric'.

Patients could be transferred from the day hospital to a social day centre whenever needed in 15 per cent of day hospitals (162 replies): 13 per cent had no day centre available and in the remaining 72 per cent it was available but access was limited.

The respondents were asked to rate six different functions of the day hospital in rank order from their point of view, and the findings were as follows.

rehabilitation

physical maintenance

nursing procedures

relief for relatives

medical procedures

other.

'Other' functions include the use of the day hospital as an out-patient consultative clinic, assessment of patients for suitability for Part III accommodation, the treatment of depression, wheel-chair clinic, the management of medicines for patients with no relatives, social activities and dealing with social problems.

Staff

From our first survey we obtained an overall picture of the numbers and grades of staff in various professions in British day hospitals in 1977.

Table 2 shows the medical staffing on the basis of sessions per week, a session being a nominal half day (that is, 2½–3 hours).

It will be seen that consultants generally spend about two sessions a week in day hospitals. In the 30 per cent which have no consultant it is probable that the clinical assistant—the next grade most commonly involved—is in charge. The clinical assistants spend much more time than consultants in day hospitals and provide most of the senior medical care. Registrars and senior house officers are on the staff of about one-third of the day hospitals, the former generally spending less time there. The figure for senior registrars is high; in 1977 there were only 69 senior registrars in geriatric medicine in the country. And it will be noted that only 18 day hospitals had medical assistants. Our figures show enormous variety in medical staffing, and the role of the different grades is discussed in Chapter 5.

Table 2 Medical staff: grades and sessions per week

	senior house officer	*registrar*	*senior registrar*	*clinical assistant*	*medical assistant*	*consultant*
day hospitals where staffing includes the grade	71 (36%)	66 (30%)	47 (22%)	112 (52%)	18 (8%)	152 (70%)
sessions per week (%)						
less than 2	27	54	68	29	33	50
2 to 4	43	30	28	36	49	49
5	23	14	4	22	6	1
6 or more	7	2	–	13	12	–

The staffing patterns for nurses, physiotherapists and occupational therapists are less varied, as Tables 3 and 4 show. Nearly all day hospitals have State registered and State enrolled nurses and qualified physiotherapists, but fewer have occupational therapists. In some hospitals, the therapist aides seem to work unsupervised.

Table 3 Nursing staff: grades and whole-time equivalents

	SRN	*SEN*	*Other*
day hospitals where staffing includes the grade	183 (84%)	153 (71%)	178 (82%)
WTE (%)			
up to 1	49	62	41
1½ to 2	39	22	33
2½ or more	12	16	26

Table 4 Physiotherapists and occupational therapists: whole-time equivalents

	physiotherapists		*occupational therapists*	
	qualified	*aide*	*qualified*	*aide*
day hospitals where staffing includes the grade	187 (86%)	133 (61%)	148 (68%)	139 (64%)
WTE (%)				
up to 1	63	56	57	48
1½ to 2	18	21	24	19
2½ or more	19	23	19	33

Only just over half the day hospitals have qualified social workers, and one-fifth have unqualified. Thus it would seem that about one-quarter of the hospitals provide no social work (see Table 5). Speech therapy and chiropody are better represented – about two-thirds of the hospitals provide these services. Hairdressers work in less than half the day hospitals, though quite a few work 2½ or more sessions a week. About one-fifth of the hospitals provide dentistry (see Table 6). Half the hospitals have a secretary and about one-third have a clerk, working part-time; and only 15 hospitals have a hostess-receptionist (see Table 7).

Table 5 Social workers: sessions per week

	qualified	*unqualified*
day hospitals where staffing includes the grade	116 (53%)	44 (20%)
sessions (%)		
1	58	53
1½ to 2	22	27
2½ or more	20	20

A long and varied list was compiled of other staff who work regularly in the day hospital, though the amount of time worked weekly cannot be accurately counted.

appliance fitter

art therapist

audiologist

barber

beautician
club organiser
community and industrial liaison officer
coordinator
counsellor (diet, finance)
day hospital or geriatric liaison officer
dietitian
diversional therapist
driver
ECG technician
laundry staff
librarian
music therapist
occupational therapy technician
optician
pharmacist
psychologist
radiographer
remedial gymnast
social activities organiser
teacher (arts, handicrafts, cookery, music and movements, yoga)
technical instructor.

To these may be added cleaners, domestic workers and porters who play a most important role in day hospital care, as do all grades of catering staff. Many of these work partly in the inpatient departments as well.

Table 6 Speech therapists, chiropodists, hairdressers and dentists: sessions per week

	*speech therapists**	*chiropodists*	*hairdressers*	*dentists*
day hospitals where staffing includes these staff	139 (64%)	136 (63%)	102 (47%)	41 (19%)
sessions (%)				
1	63	76	54	78
1½ to 2	19	17	18	17
2½ or more	18	7	28	5

*Three day hospitals employ unqualified speech therapists.

Table 7 Secretaries, clerks and receptionists: sessions per week

	secretaries	*clerks*	*receptionists (hostesses)*
day hospitals where staffing includes these staff	108 (50%)	74 (34%)	15 (7%)
sessions (%)			
1	25	18	7
1½ to 2	6	7	20
2½ or more	69	75	73

The overall impression of staffing is that about 30 per cent of day hospitals do not have the professional staff required for the work to be done, though our figures do not show to what extent deficiences of different types of staff occur in the same hospital. In two-thirds, however, most grades of staff are represented, and in about one-fifth of day hospitals the numbers of qualified staff of all grades would seem to be very good, perhaps even generous. These probably represent the 17 per cent of day hospitals with an average weekly attendance of 150 or more patients. Some of these day hospitals are also used for medical undergraduate and post-graduate training.

5
A week in the life of a day hospital

Summary

Our second survey provided information from 104 geriatric day hospitals on the work done in one week, 31 October to 5 November 1977.

The mean number of places was 31 (range 6–75), and the mean number of patients attending during the week was 114. The mean number of new patients was 4.4.

Of the 456 new patients admitted to the 104 day hospitals, 63 per cent came from the community and 37 per cent from hospital. Only 4 per cent of these new patients could have attended a social day centre.

Of the 321 patients discharged, 50 per cent had improved, 32 per cent had deteriorated, died or were admitted to hospital, and 10 per cent discharged themselves. Of the patients discharged, 17 per cent were referred to social day centres.

There were 7083 patients on the registers of the 104 hospitals. A physician saw 54 per cent of them. The nurses worked seven sessions and gave direct attention to 18 patients a day in each hospital. Physiotherapists worked, on average, less than the equivalent of one whole-time physiotherapist and treated 19 patients per day. Occupational therapists worked, on average, about the same period as the physiotherapists, treating 14 patients per day. A few patients were seen during the week by speech therapists, dietitians and social workers.

Multipurpose ambulances were most frequently used to take patients to and from the day hospitals (72 per cent), and 24 per cent of units had a special ambulance team for the day hospital. Most day hospitals had secretarial staff, generally working 9.1 sessions a week.

To obtain a picture of work carried out in geriatric day hospitals in Great Britain information was collected from a group of day hospitals–with particular reference to the numbers of staff, the type of work carried out by the staff, and the numbers of patients admitted and discharged during the week 31 October to 5 November 1977.

Of the 226 consultants who returned our first questionnaire, 140 agreed to fill in another questionnaire. Of these, 107 completed and returned the second questionnaire. Three of these could not be coded and so the figures given generally relate to 104 respondents, although not all of these answered every question.

Many of the respondents indicated that the week chosen was atypical for one reason or another. Twenty-nine drew attention to leave or sickness amongst staff which affected the work of that particular week. In four hospitals the week chosen included a non-statutory bank holiday and so they were open only four days instead of five. Three hospitals were affected by ambulance strikes, and in one case the day hospital was lodged in smaller alternative accommodation during the chosen week because of repairs to the roof.

However, these are the normal problems encountered in the management of day hospitals and it would be unrealistic to say that they created conditions which were atypical. The data are therefore presented as representing an average week in the work of British day hospitals.

It is not possible, however, to say how typical the sample is of day hospitals, of which it represents about one-third. The clinicians went to a good deal of trouble to obtain the necessary information and in that sense are a self-selected group. However, the range of day hospitals represented is so considerable that it seems unlikely that this group is significantly different from the remaining two-thirds.

There was a total of 11 819 attendances during the week—an average of 114 per day hospital. The mean number of places per day hospital was 31, which is equivalent to 1.76 places per 1000 population aged 65 and over served. The range was enormous: from 6 to 75 places. The average daily attendance over all was 23, giving a mean occupancy of 75 per cent. The mean number of new patients starting during the week was 4.4. Again, the range was considerable: from 0 to 32.

New patients

There were 456 new patients admitted: 63 per cent referred directly from general practitioners and 37 per cent on discharge from inpatient hospitals (see Table 8). The most frequent method of referral from general practitioners was by domiciliary consultation and 12 per cent were by assessment visits. The distinction between these two methods of referral is that domiciliary consultations are requested by general practitioners who are asking for advice on the management of their patients. (The domiciliary consultation is carried out by a consultant, for which he is paid a fee.) Assessment visits are initiated by the hospital when general

Table 8 Sources of and principal reasons for referral (100 per cent: 456 new patients)

Sources of referral	%
general practitioners	
by domiciliary consultation	26
outpatient clinic	20
assessment visit	12
other	5
hospital inpatient	
geriatric	28
general medicine	5
other	4
	100
Principal reasons for referral	
rehabilitation	53
assessment	20
maintenance	11
medical/nursing procedures	8
relatives' relief (social)	5
other	3
	100

practitioners request admission of their patients. (The assessment visit does not attract a fee and is not necessarily carried out by a consultant.) In practice, the distinction between these two methods of referral is not as clear as the above would suggest. For example, in an assessment visit, it is not always certain that the general practitioner had envisaged the patient's admission. Nevertheless, the fact that 12 per cent of all patients accepted for day hospital care (18 per cent of those referred by general practitioners), have been seen on assessment visits suggests that the day hospital is receiving a significant proportion of patients whom the general practitioner had thought required admission to hospital. Twenty per cent of patients had been seen initially by the consultant or his colleagues in the outpatient clinic. The great majority of inpatients referred came from geriatric wards.

Since 37 per cent of new patients had been inpatients, presumably many of them came for continuing rehabilitation. It is difficult to be precise about individual geriatricians' interpretation of the terms used and no qualifying statement was added in the questionnaire. Geriatricians regard rehabilitation as the most important aspect of day hospital care, but in Brocklehurst's 1970 survey they ranked physical maintenance as almost equally important.[12]

In the present survey, only four per cent of the newly admitted patients could equally well have attended a social day centre in the consultants' opinions.

Most patients attended the day hospital on one or two days of the week (47 per cent on one day and 41 per cent on two). Only three per cent were under 65 years old.

Patients discharged

Table 9 shows the reasons for discharge. In the 104 day hospitals, 53 patients were referred to social day centres: 17 per cent of the total and 33 per cent of those discharged as improved. The latter are the only ones likely to be suitable for day centres.

Medical work

The medical staff saw 3817 patients. This represents 32 per cent of all attendances during the week, but 54 per cent of the 7083

Table 9 Reasons for discharge (100 per cent: 321 patients)

	%
improved	50
deteriorated, admitted to hospital or died	32
did not want to continue	10
other	8
	100

patients actually on the registers of the day hospitals at that time. Probably not all registered patients attended during the week and so the percentage of individual patients seen by physicians is likely to be greater than 54 per cent. The medical staff worked 538 sessions during the week: consultants, 22 per cent; senior registrars or medical assistants, 30 per cent; registrars, senior house officers, preregistration house officers, 25 per cent; general practitioners, 23 per cent.

This suggests that seven patients were seen in a session, but this could be a low figure since many of the consultants' sessions were probably case conferences in which at least one other member of the medical staff would be present. It is interesting that almost one-quarter of the time of the medical staff was given by general practitioners acting as clinical assistants with responsibility for all patients attending, not necessarily those on the general practitioners' own lists.

More consultants (80 per cent) were involved in the 104 day hospitals than in the 217 hospitals in the first survey (70 per cent), and fewer clinical assistants (37 per cent compared with 52 per cent.* It is probable that the consultants completing the second questionnaire were the ones more interested in day hospitals. Although more consultants are involved, on the whole they spend rather less time in the day hospital (66 per cent fewer than two sessions a week compared with 50 per cent in the first survey).

The proportions of time spent in different activities by all grades of medical staff were as follows.

examining/consulting (other than case conferences) 60 per cent

multidisciplinary case conferences 16 per cent

administration 13 per cent

practical procedures other than examination 7 per cent

teaching in the day hospital 4 per cent.

In general it is likely that most of the consultant's time is devoted to case conferences, teaching and some administration, and most of the time of the rest of the medical staff in examining and talking to patients and in practical procedures.

The consultants were asked about the types of practical procedures carried out during the week, but only 40 replied in detail. However, these give some indication of the relative frequency of practical procedures.

syringing ears 36

sigmoidoscopy or proctoscopy 15

*See Table 2, page 41.

bone biopsy 3

bone marrow aspiration 1

pessary insertion 1

transfusion 1

These procedures were enquired about specifically, but the consultants were invited to mention any others. The commonest were electrocardiograph (6) and venepuncture (7).

Other specialists saw patients during the week.

dentist 422 (6 per cent of registered patients)

ophthalmologist 13 (0.2 per cent)

otorhinolaryngologist 5 (0.07 per cent).

Nursing work

Replies from 101 day hospitals showed that nurses attended 9330 patients (an average of 92 patients per week, or 18 patients per day). The nurses, in all grades, worked a total of 3490 sessions (an average of 35 per week or seven sessions per day, that is, 3.5 nurses each day). This gives an average of five patients per nurse per day. In addition to direct work for individual patients, nurses are responsible for the general care of all patients–receiving them from the ambulance, supervising their movements around the day hospital, their meals, the arrangement of clinics and so on.

Of the total of 3490 sessions worked, 33 per cent were by State registered nurses, 27 per cent by State enrolled nurses and 40 per cent by auxiliary nurses. From these figures it appears that the average day hospital had State registered nurses working for 11 sessions, or one whole-time equivalent.

Percentages of time were spent as follows.

supportive (toilet, washing) 58

administration 18

technical procedures 16

attendance at case conferences 5

teaching 3

The nursing time spent in the day hospital is 6.5 times that of medical time, and in comparing time spent in case conferences it would appear that two nurses attend these to every one doctor.

Specified nursing procedures were carried out on 7257 occasions; that is, on average 0.8 of a procedure per patient per week, or 80 per cent of patients having one procedure during the week. No doubt, however, in many cases two or more procedures were carried out for the same patient. The procedures, expressed in percentages, were as follows.

bathing 28

taking blood pressure 18

dressings 12

treatment of ulcers 11

collecting mid-stream specimen of urine 8

taking blood samples 7

enemata 4

injections 4

changing catheter 1

bladder washout 1

other 6

Since these replies relate to 101 day hospitals, they indicate an average of 72 practical nursing procedures per week, or 14 per day. The number of baths given is very striking–an average of 19 a week or four a day. Measurement of blood pressure was the next most frequent procedure. On the other hand, the number of enemata given would seem to be small, approximately three per week. The number of catheter changes and bladder washouts is less than one per week.

Other technical procedures were syringing ears, ECG, washing patients' clothes, toilet training, oral hygiene, attending to colostomy and weighing patients.

There seems to be some interchangeability between nursing and medical staff as far as syringing ears and taking blood samples are concerned, although in some areas nurses are not allowed to undertake venepuncture.

Physiotherapists

In 97 day hospitals, physiotherapists treated 5655 patients during the week (an average of 58 patients per week, or 19 patients per day). This represents a total of 51 per cent of all patients attending and 85 per cent of all patients registered. Trained physiotherapists worked an average of 7½ sessions and aides worked 6, both less than one whole-time equivalent.

Percentages of time were spent as follows.

practical procedures 76

administration 12

case conferences 6

teaching 3

making and fitting splints and appliances 2

home assessment 1

The practical procedures are considered in relation to the percentage of day hospitals in which they were undertaken and thus give some indication of the importance attached to them.

active movements 98

passive movements 91

heat, ultraviolet light, shortwave diathermy 85

group physical therapy 75

fitting and preparing splints and other appliances 53

Other procedures reported in some day hospitals were Bobath exercises (proprioceptive neuromuscular facilitation techniques), breathing exercises, wheelchair assessment and exercises, suspension procedures using pulleys and slings, and the use of wax baths, but the proportion of day hospitals using these various techniques was not assessed.

Occupational therapists

The work of occupational therapists was obtained from 96 day hospitals: 6730 patients were attended (an average of 70 patients per week or 14 per day). This represents an average of 61 per cent of all patients attending and 96 per cent of all patients registered. Trained staff worked an average eight sessions per week and aides worked 11. These figures, and those from the first survey, show that more occupational therapists and aides are employed in day hospitals than are physiotherapists and aides.

They spent similar times in the various activities (expressed in percentages).

practical procedures 57

administration 17

preparing and finishing work 13

case conferences 6

teaching 4

home assessment 3

Practical procedures are again expressed in percentages in relation to the day hospitals in which they are performed.

preparing and finishing work 94

aids to daily living (ADL) 89

individual remedial therapy 88

ADL assessment 86

group remedial therapy 79

assessment of spatial orientation of patients with strokes 45

We were interested to see that only half the physiotherapists fit and prepare splints and other appliances, and rather less than half the occupational therapists assess spatial orientation in patients with stroke. Both these would seem to be important aspects of geriatric practice. It is also worth noting that in 85 per cent of physiotherapy departments in day hospitals, heat, shortwave diathermy, ultraviolet light and similar treatments are used.

Speech therapists

Only 68 day hospitals gave information about speech therapists. They attended 363 patients during the week (an average of 5.3 patients per day hospital). Speech therapy was involved in the case of only five per cent of the total number of patients attending these day hospitals. Eight per cent of all registered patients saw a speech therapist. In a few other day hospitals it was noted that speech therapists were 'available as required' but did not attend regularly. In the 68 day hospitals, the average number of sessions worked by trained speech therapists was 1.75, with 0.15 session by an aide.

The percentages of time spent by trained speech therapists were as follows.

procedures with patients 77

administration 10

teaching 7

case conferences 6

The percentages of day hospitals in which different speech therapy procedures were employed were as follows.

individual treatment 93

assessment 68

group treatment 32

Dietitians

Even fewer day hospitals (28) gave information on dietitians. Altogether they saw 506 patients during the week (an average of 18 patients for each dietitian, or 16 per cent of the total patients attending, and 26 per cent of patients registered). Some of the other day hospitals indicated that dietitians were 'available on request' but were not part of the regular staff. In the 28 day hospitals, the dietitian spent an average of 1.1 sessions a week and dietetic aids were available for 0.4 session weekly.

They spent their time (percentages) as follows.

with patients or relatives, teaching and advising 74

administration 15

food preparation 6

case conferences 4

teaching staff 1

The main indications for their advice were diabetes and obesity (both in 93 per cent of the day hospitals). Anaemia and malnutrition were rather less frequent reasons for advice. Other reasons given were renal failure and coeliac disease (each in one case only).

Social workers

Information about social workers was given by 74 day hospitals, and in these 526 patients were seen (7.1 patients per day hospital, or a total of 6 per cent of all patients attending and 10 per cent of all patients registered at the 74 day hospitals that week). In addition, however, the social workers spent an average of six hours of the week outside the hospital, dealing with the affairs of the day hospital patients.

The numbers of staff employed for day hospital patients on a sessional basis were as follows.

trained staff 1.9 sessions

untrained staff 0.5 session

social work assistants 0.6 session

This gives a total of three sessions of social work time to the average day hospital.

The percentages of time spent in different activities were as follows.

with patients or relatives in the day hospital or an adjoining office 34

home visits 30

administration 23

case conferences 12

teaching 1

Their work with and for patients comprised interviews (including interviews with relatives), home assessments, arranging living accommodation and organising services.

The other 30 day hospitals had no social worker regularly in attendance. A few normally had a social worker but she was not available during the week of the survey and a larger number used social workers from the inpatient hospitals or local authorities from time to time as required.

Administrative and secretarial staff

Information about administrative and secretarial staff was obtained from 95 day hospitals, 84 of which (88 per cent) had their own secretarial staff. In these 84 units, there were 768 sessions of administrative and secretarial staff time—an average of 9.1 sessions per day hospital. Sixty-eight per cent of these sessions were for a personal secretary or shorthand typist, 18 per cent were for staff of the higher clerical grade and 14 per cent for the administrative grade. In most cases, staff of the administrative or higher clerical grade worked for one-half to two sessions. A few hospitals had an administrator or higher clerical grade officer working whole-time. Seventeen per cent of day hospitals had some sessions from higher clerical grade officers, and 17 per cent had some sessions from the administrator grade. In the great majority, the clerical service was provided by a personal secretary or shorthand typist.

Transport

Replies on transport by ambulance came from 102 day hospitals. In the other two the ambulancemen were on strike during the week surveyed.

The types of vehicles used to bring the patients in were (in percentages)

multipurpose ambulances (used also for emergencies) 72

sitting type vehicle 14

special vehicle for day hospital only 6

private transport (car or taxi) 4

voluntary transport or social services vehicle 3

taxi paid for by NHS 1

The heavy use of multipurpose vehicles is discussed further in Chapter 9.

Ninety-six hospitals responded to the question on whether there was a special ambulance team for the day hospital; 23 said they had.

Porters

Ninety-five day hospitals gave information about porters: they had an average of 12 hours of portering time per week; 56 per cent of this time was spent with patients and 44 per cent in other work for the day hospital.

Domestic staff

Ninety-seven hospitals referred to domestic staff, and in these the average number of hours worked was 45 per week.

Other staff

Chiropodists saw 422 patients in the day hospitals involved in this second survey: 4 per cent of all patients attending and 6 per cent of registered patients. A hairdresser attended 588 patients (5 per cent of all patients attending and 8 per cent of registered patients).

Table 10 gives an idea of the amount of contact which the various professional staff had with patients during the week. The table excludes nursing staff who, of course, have continuous contact.

Table 10 Patient–staff contacts

	proportion of patients attending	*proportion of patients registered*
	%	%
occupational therapist	61	96
physiotherapist	51	85
doctor	32	54
dietitian	16	26
social worker	6	10
speech therapist	5	8
chiropodist	4	6

6

Operational policy and management

Summary

This chapter describes the views of staff on the purpose, policy, management and work of geriatric day hospitals, and their relationship to other geriatric services and to the local general practitioners. The information was collected during visits to the 30 day hospitals listed in the Appendix. The numbers of staff of the various professions who were interviewed are discussed in Chapter 2. The chief purpose of the day hospital was felt by 41 per cent of all staff to be active treatment of patients; by 19 per cent to be maintenance of patients. Only 2 per cent felt that the chief purpose was social, and 38 per cent felt that the hospital combined all these purposes. Those working in adapted rather than purpose-built premises were less inclined to feel that active treatment was the chief purpose.

In all the hospitals a consultant geriatrician was in overall charge. A nurse was in day-to-day charge in 21 hospitals; in the remainder it was another member of staff or a team.

Ten hospitals were the main centre for rehabilitation of inpatients and three served as the outpatient department of the geriatric unit.

Referrals were accepted only from doctors by 25 day hospitals, the others would accept referrals also from paramedical staff.

Only five hospitals had a waiting list, and in two the waiting period was more than a month. Eight hospitals had a referral form; in the rest referral was essentially informal and nearly all the hospitals had informal programming meetings.

Most staff (70 per cent) thought the patients were not fully occupied but that it would be inappropriate to try to increase their activity. Some staff (16 per cent) thought the treatment offered was inadequate.

All but six of the 30 hospitals had regular case conferences or a 'ward round' led by the consultant geriatrician. Usually the case conferences were not attended by the patient concerned. Half the hospitals undertook teaching, mainly of student nurses. A few were used for teaching medical students and student remedial therapists.

Eleven hospitals provided separate facilities for psychogeriatric patients. Ten others accepted patients whose primary diagnosis was dementia; nine hospitals did not accept these patients and nearly all the staff of the 30 hospitals felt that demented patients required separate facilities.

Eighteen hospitals prescribed drugs and some used the treatment cards as a means of contact with the patient's general practitioner.

Most of the staff felt their contact with community services was satisfactory, though formal meetings with community health workers were held in only seven hospitals.

Purpose

Table 11 shows, in percentages, the views of staff in both adapted and purpose-built premises. We shall comment on the main

Table 11 Views of staff on the purpose of a geriatric day hospital

	physicians	*nurses*	*physio-therapists*	*occupational therapists*	*social workers*	*all staff*
In adapted premises	%	%	%	%	%	%
active rehabilitation	46	13	40	22	–	27
physical maintenance	38	26	13	33	25	27
social	–	7	13	–	–	5
combined purpose	16	54	34	45	75	41
In purpose-built hospitals						
active rehabilitation	64	47	74	53	–	54
physical maintenance	18	20	13	–	–	12
social	–	–	–	–	–	–
combined purpose	18	33	13	47	100	34
In all hospitals						
active rehabilitation	56	30	56	42	–	41
physical maintenance	27	23	13	8	24	19
social	–	3	7	–	–	2
combined purpose	17	44	24	50	76	38
number interviewed	30	30	30	24	14	128

features and report other findings not shown in the table, comparing the views of the present with some of those of the past.

Forty-one per cent of staff regarded the main purpose of the day hospital as that of an active treatment centre offering rehabilitation and medical and nursing care. There was, however, some variation between groups. Rather fewer nurses (30 per cent) and occupational therapists (42 per cent) took this view than physicians and physiotherapists (both 56 per cent). Nineteen per cent of all the staff saw the day hospital as primarily a unit for physical maintenance of disabled patients. More nurses were inclined to this view than the remedial staff. Only one nurse and two physiotherapists saw the day hospital as essentially a social centre. Quite a large percentage (38) felt the day hospital had a combined purpose of active treatment, physical maintenance and social care and were all equally important. Social workers (76 per cent), occupational therapists (50 per cent) and nurses (44 per cent) were particularly inclined to this combined role.

An important difference of opinion was expressed by staff working in day hospitals using adapted buildings and those in purpose-built hospitals. Only 27 per cent of the staff working in adapted premises felt that active treatment was the chief purpose compared with 54 per cent of those working in purpose-built day hospitals. Staff in the adapted day hospitals gave higher priority to physical maintenance. The three staff members who saw the unit as primarily a social centre worked in adapted premises. Presumably these differences reflect the better facilities for active rehabilitation and medical and nursing care in the purpose-built hospitals. Similar percentages of staff in both kinds of premises thought that the day hospital's purpose was a combination of active treatment, physical maintenance and social care, with no particular priority given to any one of these.

There was fairly close agreement about purpose between doctors, nurses and remedial staff working in any one day hospital. This suggests a common policy and approach. The group who looked at things rather differently was the social workers, most of whom felt that the day hospital should have a combined purpose. Interestingly, none of them thought the day hospital was primarily a social centre.

Our findings indicate the change of emphasis about purpose. In earlier years, day hospitals were perhaps more oriented towards physical maintenance and social care than active rehabilitation and medical and nursing care. Cosin (1954) described the role of the day hospital in supporting and maintaining elderly infirm and confused patients in the community.[17] And Droller described his policy for discharging geriatric outpatients as 'conservative. If there is any chance of social breakdown we prefer to keep them.'[21] Farndale, in 1961, saw a distinct similarity between day hospitals for infirm people and day centres, the types of patient attending them, the needs of the old people, and the types of treatment and occupation offered. He thought there was a need for further research and some clear thinking on the purpose of a day hospital for old people.[26] Fine (1964) described the purpose of a day hospital as maintenance of the independence of old people by sharing the responsibility of care with the family.[27] Woodford-Williams and Alvarez stated that the aims of the day hospital were to provide economy in the use of beds, rehabilitation and supervision in medical care, long-term social supervision and the stimulation of apathetic or inadequate personalities, the relief of social isolation and depression, and of strain on relatives.[80] Andrews, Fairley and Hyland wrote in 1970 that the geriatric day hospital should be a centre for medical investigation and treatment with the full range of rehabilitation services. They stated firmly, 'It is in no sense a holding unit, and should not be confused with the day centre—provision of which is the responsibility of the local authority.'[3]

Brocklehurst (1970) found rehabilitation rated as the most important function of the day hospital, with physical maintenance having lower priority and purely social care coming last.[12]

The DHSS circular of 1971 stated

> 'Day hospital functions are rehabilitation of the elderly who may have been ill, and, by active treatment and supervision, maintaining independence when threatened. It may also be useful for the assessment of those patients who do not need to be admitted for this purpose, but who cannot be adequately assessed at home or at an out-patient consultation.'[31]

Thus it seems that the policy of active treatment has gradually become accepted as the most important purpose of the day hospital, with a much clearer distinction between day hospitals and day centres.

To what extent are day hospitals fulfilling their purpose? All the staff interviewed in the present survey were asked this. Their views are shown in Table 12. It will be seen that most thought their own hospital was working well and functioning as it should; 24 per cent had some reservations, mainly about the number of patients coming for physical maintenance and social reasons which was higher than they felt was appropriate. Only two physiotherapists and one occupational therapist thought their day hospital was not fulfilling its purpose, and all three worked in purpose-built day hospitals. They felt very strongly that, whilst their facilities were good for treating patients, these were not being fully used. In general the remedial staff had more doubts than had other workers. The nurses and social workers seemed to be most confident that the day hospital was doing its job. We noticed again the difference of the views of staff in purpose-built hospitals and of those in adapted premises.

Table 12 Views of staff on whether the day hospital fulfilled its purpose

	physicians	*nurses*	*physio-therapists*	*occupational therapists*	*social workers*	*all staff*
In adapted premises	%	%	%	%	%	%
yes	62	80	53	66	75	66
no	–	–	–	–	–	–
equivocal	38	20	47	34	25	34
In purpose-built hospitals						
yes	88	87	66	73	100	81
no	–	–	13	7	–	4
equivocal	12	13	21	20	–	15
In all hospitals						
yes	76	83	60	71	86	74
no	–	–	7	4	–	2
equivocal	24	17	33	25	14	24
number interviewed	30	30	30	24	14	128

Who is in charge?

A consultant physician in geriatric medicine must be in overall charge. In all 30 hospitals this was so, although in some the consultant's responsibility was essentially administrative, clinical management being completely in the hands of another physician, usually a clinical assistant or senior registrar.

Seventeen hospitals were managed by one consultant, often because there was only one consultant in the health district. In others one member of the team of consultants in the health district had responsibility for the day hospital. Usually this overall responsibility was administrative rather than clinical, but in two hospitals one consultant looked after all the patients whether they had been referred by himself or by one of his colleagues.

In the other 13 hospitals, administrative responsibility for the day hospital was shared by all the consultant geriatricians in the health district. Both of these arrangements had their advocates. Many of the staff interviewed felt it was useful for the paramedical team to be able to relate to just one consultant. In three of the day hospitals with more than one consultant in charge, several members of the staff felt that this caused difficulties. The consultants may well have different policies about their patients, and the nurses and remedial staff would then have the problem of implementing one policy for one group of patients and a different policy for another. The same arguments have been advanced in favour of having one consultant in charge of an inpatient ward. One solution in the day hospital, if there are enough staff, would be for each consultant to have his own nursing, remedial and social work team who would work only with his patients. Some of the larger day hospitals had attempted to develop such an arrangement but often it was limited by staff shortages.

Perhaps more important than the question of overall responsibility is that of who should be in day-to-day charge. It must be someone working solely in the day hospital and this excludes most hospital doctors, who have many other commitments. In many day hospitals it also excludes remedial staff whose responsibilities are divided between the day hospital and the wards. In most day hospitals, it seemed to be accepted that a nursing sister or charge nurse working full-time in the day hospital was the best person to be in day-to-day charge. However, in some of the larger day hospitals with full-time remedial staff, physiotherapists and occupational therapists were not entirely happy about having a nurse in charge. They thought that since the unit was primarily a rehabilitation unit a remedial therapist might more appropriately be in charge. Some nurses, on the other hand, considered that their traditionally close links with the medical staff put them in the best position to run the day hospital. The personalities of the individuals involved are most important factors here, and in most instances remedial staff seemed quite happy to have a nurse in charge provided she did not also try to run their departments. Discussing this question, Greenfield (1974) thought that the most appropriate person to be in charge would vary from place to place and that this should perhaps depend on the people available to fulfil this role than on traditional hospital practice.[33]

In 21 of the hospitals visited a nursing sister was in charge; in the remaining nine another member of staff was seen as being in charge, or the responsibility was being jointly undertaken by various members of staff. In the few day hospitals where no one was seen as being in charge, all the staff seemed highly satisfied with the arrangement. They felt that conflict was less likely if the nurse was simply in charge of nursing, and the remedial staff in charge of their departments. These hospitals all had a clerical officer who was responsible for coordinating appointments, transport and so on, and it could fairly be said that the smooth running of the day hospital depended largely on her.

A remedial therapist was in day-to-day charge in only three hospitals. One of these was a combination of day hospital and day centre, and although the organiser was by training an occupational therapist, her predecessors had had different backgrounds. In another hospital a physiotherapist was in charge, essentially because she happened to be the dominant personality among the staff. She was in charge unofficially, but unequivocally.

In four day hospitals the person in day-to-day charge was a physician, either a clinical assistant with five or more sessions in the day hospital or a senior hospital medical officer who spent much of his time there. In one of these hospitals, the other members of staff thought it an ideal arrangement to have a physician who was in attendance most of the time and was able to co-ordinate and organise activities. They felt that only a physician could run the unit and relate satisfactorily to the other members of staff without arousing any conflicts.

Brocklehurst in his national survey in 1970 found that 80 per cent of day hospitals had a particular staff member in charge, working under the consultant's direction; in 68 per cent this was a nurse, and in 22 per cent an occupational therapist.[12]

We draw no firm conclusions on who is the best person to take charge of the day-to-day running of the day hospital. It depends entirely on the local circumstances and the calibre of staff in the various disciplines. It may be said, though, that adherence to tradition may be inappropriate and that the best person to run the day hospital should be the best person available at the time.

How should day hospitals relate to other hospital services?

Most of the day hospitals visited were primarily concerned with outpatient service. Some had a few inpatients attending, usually just before their discharge, to help them get used to ordinary life again. Only ten hospitals were used also as the main centres for geriatric inpatient rehabilitation—a rather smaller number than expected. Sometimes this was because the location of the day hospital was such that few inpatients would benefit from treatment there. Often it was because facilities for rehabilitation in the day hospital were not adequate for inpatients as well as for outpatients. In others rehabilitation facilities provided separately for inpatients were adequate and there was no need to use the day hospital to treat them. Where the day hospital was the rehabilitation centre for both inpatients and outpatients, staff felt that there were many advantages to this approach. It avoided duplication of services, and allowed inpatients and outpatients to reap the benefits of being treated together. The benefits were thought to be particularly important for the inpatients who would meet others, equally disabled, who were coping well enough and would be encouraged by them. Such a day hospital is more likely to be a central and vital part of the activities of the geriatric department than one which serves only outpatients and works in isolation from the rehabilitation service for inpatients.

The idea of the day hospital as the hub of the geriatric service has been taken further in three day hospitals which also serve as the outpatient department for the geriatric unit. This has mainly arisen out of necessity because there were no other outpatient facilities. At least one consultant, however, emphasised the usefulness of being able to assess an outpatient in his clinic in the normal way and then if necessary pass him straight over to the remedial staff for their assessment. It was also suggested that, provided all the investigation facilities were near at hand, it was a great deal pleasanter for the elderly patient to attend a day hospital for the day for assessment, investigation and treatment as necessary than to be thrown into the chaos of the average general outpatient department where the pace would be much more hectic, no meal would be available at midday, and nursing and other staff might not be particularly oriented towards the needs of the elderly. One consultant, who had started a geriatric day hospital in adapted premises (a room next to the physiotherapy and occupational therapy departments) and currently held his outpatient clinic in the main outpatient department, said that plans for his new purpose-built day hospital were to include an outpatient suite. He considered this would be a major improvement: his outpatients would be more relaxed and less confused.

Our impression of these three day hospitals, where outpatients were being seen, day hospital patients were being rehabilitated and inpatients were coming for treatment, was that there was just a little bit too much going on. The individual patient may have tended to become lost. One possible compromise would be to have a separate outpatient suite, adjacent to the day hospital, so that the few outpatients who needed it could spend a whole day there and be assessed by the remedial therapists, and have their midday meal and a tea or coffee break.

Other day hospitals have developed specialised clinics. For example, Irvine (1969) described a wheelchair clinic in the day hospital at Hastings, in which the appropriate wheelchair for a patient can be assessed.[40]

In practice the precise role of the day hospital in relation to inpatient services will depend on its situation and access to investigational facilities. Some day hospitals will be in the right position to act as the centre of the geriatric service; others will have to take a more peripheral role. Pathy (1969) has described how three day hospitals in Cardiff complement one another, one has access to full investigational facilities and can offer full medical supervision; another, situated more peripherally, offers routine rehabilitation; and the third is attached to a long-stay unit and offers longer-term day care.[59] Such a three-tier system would certainly have advantages in helping to meet the particular needs of individual patients, provided that it was economically possible.

Referrals

In 25 day hospitals patients were referred only by a physician; usually the consultant geriatrician or his senior registrar referred patients seen at outpatient clinics, in domiciliary consultations, on discharge from the geriatric unit, and, sometimes, from other wards of the hospital. Only three day hospitals accepted patients directly referred to them from medical staff outside the geriatric unit. Where patients referred by general practitioners were accepted, there seemed to be a feeling amongst the paramedical staff in the day hospital that some of the referrals were inappropriate. That one might expect this to be so is suggested by the information obtained by Hildick-Smith's survey. She found that general practitioners were equally likely to refer patients to the day hospital who were fit but causing family tension as patients who needed active rehabilitation. She also found a good deal of confusion amongst general practitioners about the distinction between day hospitals and day centres, but this was partly because the area had little provision of social day care.*

Most of the consultants we interviewed welcomed referral from general practitioners, specifically mentioning that they found day hospital care to be appropriate for the patients who were referred, but they liked to assess the patient themselves first, either at an outpatient clinic or on a domiciliary visit. In one day hospital consultants other than geriatricians were invited to refer patients directly for day hospital treatment, and here the staff thought that most of the patients were appropriately referred. Usually, the referrals came from housemen and orthopaedic surgeons.

Five day hospitals accepted referrals from sources other than a physician. Three of these functioned as combined day hospitals and day centres, and accepted referrals from community social workers. These 'social services clients' were a distinct group.

*See footnote, page 12.

While they had access to the treatment facilities of the day hospital, including medical supervision if necessary, they were generally regarded as a category separate from the day hospital patients. The two other day hospitals invited other community workers to refer patients directly. This had recently been introduced as an experiment in one hospital but in the other it was established practice in which patients could be referred directly by one or more members of a 'crisis team' of medical and paramedical workers whose role was to intervene quickly when an elderly person in the community developed serious medical or social problems. The concept was pioneered at Warrington General Hospital by Dr G Davies and is said in many instances to prevent unnecessary hospital admission, by cutting the corners of the normal referral system whereby a patient comes from a general practitioner to a consultant geriatrician and then back again to community workers. A patient might be referred to the day hospital by a member of the team trained in social work, nursing or remedial therapy.

Both the day hospitals which accepted direct referral of patients had at least one member of the staff who doubted the appropriateness of some of the referrals. Most of the physicians with whom we discussed the question of referral to the day hospital by health visitors, community nurses, social workers and others felt that, although this might be a good idea, it would in practice lead to inappropriate use of scarce facilities.

Waiting lists

Most of the consultants regarded a waiting list as an admission that the day hospital was not working properly. There was no waiting list in 25 of the day hospitals we visited. Patients referred were usually able to start treatment the following week or the same week. Sometimes it was possible to arrange treatment to begin the day after the patient was referred, but in general the consultants felt that such a patient would be more appropriately taken as an inpatient.

Five day hospitals had a waiting list. In all of them the staff regarded physical maintenance, social care and relief of relatives as their prime functions, and in only two was the waiting period longer than one month. One day hospital had a waiting period of more than three months but this was partly due to difficulties with transport. The consultants there were very concerned to reduce the waiting period to a more acceptable level.

Programming referrals

In most instances, information about the patient was sent to the day hospital by letter or memorandum from the referring geriatrician. Sometimes, the referral was made by telephone, but the doctor would usually follow this up with a note detailing the background information, the reason for attendance and the treatment required. This informal referral system was used by 22 hospitals and most of the staff felt it worked satisfactorily, although some paramedical staff, particularly remedial therapists, said that guidance given to them on referral was sometimes inadequate. Eight hospitals—all large units with several geriatricians referring—had a referral form specifying details of the patients' medical and social background, and of the treatment regime required. There was some feeling that this more formal system was necessary to encourage uniformity of approach amongst the referring geriatricians and to ensure that staff in the day hospital had adequate information to plan the treatment.

In most of the day hospitals paramedical staff met at least weekly to plan a programme for each patient. The details of the planning varied considerably: a few day hospitals used the programming meeting largely as a general forum and offered all patients virtually the same 'package' of treatment; others planned each patient's regime in great detail so that it was known when every patient would be having individual physiotherapy, group therapy, occupational therapy, seeing the physician and so on. One hospital had a large board showing the treatment being received by each patient, and a similar system was suggested by some therapists and nurses working at other hospitals. They thought that a simple blackboard detailing the timing of treatment for each patient attending that day would be very useful in the larger day hospitals.

In general, programming meetings were attended by a doctor only where there was a clinical assistant or senior hospital medical officer mainly committed to the day hospital; otherwise the paramedical staff relied on the written guidance of the referring doctor.

Structure of the patients' day

The patients' day followed a similar pattern in most of the day hospitals visited. Soon after arrival, patients were greeted with a hot drink before starting their treatment or diversional work. Lunch was served around midday and treatment or diversional work was resumed in the afternoon, with a tea break.

One of the commonly voiced criticisms of day care for old people is that they are not given enough to do and spend most of the time sitting around staring into space. We asked the staff if they thought their patients had enough to do. Only 10 per cent of the staff interviewed thought the day was fully occupied but 70 per cent said that although the day was not fully occupied, the patients were getting adequate treatment and needed several rest periods between treatment sessions when no activities were planned.

Sixteen per cent of the staff thought that treatment was inadequate, generally because there were not enough remedial staff. Only four per cent of the staff interviewed felt that there was too little diversional therapy and that consequently patients spent too much time doing absolutely nothing. All the staff of this opinion were from two hospitals where staffing was a big problem, but they seemed to be making a genuine attempt to make things better for the patients.

There was no significant difference in the replies to this question from staff working in adapted premises and those working in purpose-built day hospitals. Further, there was general agreement between physicians and paramedical staff in each hospital about the nature of the patients' day.

Case conferences and review of patients

Twenty-four day hospitals were visited regularly by a consultant geriatrician. In some instances, particularly in the smaller hospitals, the visit took the form of a 'ward round' rather than a case conference. In five instances, the consultant's visit did not occupy a whole session but was part of a weekly visit to the main inpatient hospital. In two hospitals, the consultant did not visit regularly, but a senior registrar did a weekly session there. In four others there was no regular visit by a consultant; these were four which also operated without any sessions from a clinical assistant or senior hospital medical officer. Junior medical staff were available to see patients as required and the consultant would see patients on request.

Where a regular session by a consultant or senior registrar was held in the day hospital, this usually took place weekly. In three hospitals the session was once a month, and in one hospital once in three months. The hospitals with infrequent or no regular consultant sessions were mainly the longer-stay units. It often seemed that in these units the consultant was single-handed, with many other commitments, and simply did not have the time to pay a regular visit to the day hospital. The single consultant post in one health district was vacant. Where consultants were not able to visit regularly, this was always regretted by the consultant concerned and by the other staff in the day hospital. They all felt that the unit would be much more active if regular case conferences could be held.

Attendance at case conferences varied considerably. In the larger hospitals with full-time staff in most disciplines it was generally possible for doctors, nurses, occupational therapists and social workers—at least one of each—to attend. In others, mainly the smaller hospitals, only doctors and nurses attended and they generally felt that the case conferences were less satisfactory. Most of the part-time remedial therapists who were unable to attend case conferences regretted this, although some said that they had so many commitments that attending all the rounds and conferences would mean that they were unable to get on with their work. Some staff in the larger day hospitals also made this point. Where there were several consultants all holding their own day hospital clinic, the paramedical staff could spend a considerable proportion of their time at conferences unless there were enough of them to divide up into clinical teams, each under one consultant. One solution to this problem, used at three day hospitals, was for two consultants to hold their day hospital case conferences together so that patients under the care of either of them could be discussed at the same time.

Rather strikingly, in 21 of the day hospitals where regular case conferences were held the patient was not present to give his point of view. Where the consultant's session took the form of a ward round usually a few selected patients were seen, but others were discussed without being seen. In Manchester, the practice at the case conference is for a patient to be presented by the junior doctor involved in his care; the case is then discussed among all the staff, and the patient is brought in to take part in the review. Most staff at day hospitals where patients were discussed but not seen at case conferences took the view that these sessions were primarily for review rather than for medical assessment, and that any patients who required the consultant's opinion on their condition could be seen and examined after the conference. Our feeling is that if important decisions about the patient's management, including changes in the frequency of attendance at the day hospital, or perhaps discharge, are to be made at the case conference, it is essential for the patient to express his views at the time. In any case, this session may be the only opportunity the patient has to see and question his consultant.

There seems little doubt that regular consultant sessions, whether they take the form of a formal case conference or a ward round, are crucial in determining whether the day hospital operates as an active treatment centre or not. Local circumstances determine the form which this session should take, but where possible it should include representatives of all the paramedical disciplines without consuming too much of their time.

Teaching

The main function of the day hospital must always be the treatment of patients, but this presents a golden opportunity for multidisciplinary teaching. Half the day hospitals visited were involved in some kind of teaching (other than having occasional groups of community workers for a teaching visit). Thirteen of these hospitals had student nurses attached for a variable period, and this gave an opportunity for them to learn more about the role and techniques of the physiotherapist and occupational therapist. The period of attachment was often very short—sometimes only one day.

Seven hospitals involved in teaching had visits from medical students, usually for only one short session and usually to have the purpose of the day hospital explained to them rather than to become involved in seeing patients there. Sometimes medical students participated in case conferences–a useful teaching method.

Only three hospitals had physiotherapy students, and only two had occupational therapy students. There seems to be scope for much more involvement in day hospitals by students of remedial therapy. It would help them to appreciate the value of the multi-disciplinary approach, and encourage them to work in geriatric day hospitals on completion of training.

It has been suggested (Porter 1974) that as many members of staff as possible from the geriatric services in the area should rotate through day hospitals both before and after qualification, because if the unit is an active one this may well be beneficial for its morale.[61]

Psychogeriatric day care

Eleven day hospitals were in localities with other facilities for the care of severely mentally infirm old people. Sometimes they were accepted in small numbers at psychiatric day hospitals; more commonly there was a separate day hospital specifically for psychogeriatric patients. Where there were no such facilities–nine day hospitals–47 per cent of the staff accepted that day care for confused elderly patients was one of their functions, and the other 53 per cent did not.

But staff in almost all day hospitals visited felt that demented patients should be looked after in a different day hospital because their needs were completely different from those of the disabled elderly patients who were mentally sound. Many thought that confused patients upset the mentally sound patients and said that a day hospital catering for both kinds of patients had to keep the number of confused patients very low. Arie (1975) stated that more information was required on the pros and cons of mixing the two kinds of patient in one unit.[4] There are economic advantages in doing so, but most physicians and nurses interviewed felt that these were outweighed by the disadvantages to both kinds of patient. One compromise may be to have the two kinds of patient looked after in a unit designed physically to separate them for most of the day. Presumably some facilities would need to be shared and the unit might well have to be of such a size that management became difficult.

Very few of the day hospitals visited seemed to have problems with ambulant dements. Either they were very few or the day hospital was geared to their care. Many staff said that the design of the day hospital was such that demented patients, who were prone to wander, could not be looked after in safety there (too many doors or inadequate facilities for observation). In two hospitals, the geriatrician praised the psychogeriatric service, saying that the two services complemented each other satisfactorily and that patients could be referred between the two when necessary.

General practitioners

The patient attending the day hospital often seems to fall between two stools of medical care. On the one hand, he is attending the day hospital regularly, often for medical supervision, and on the other, since he is living at home, he is still very much under the care of his general practitioner. Almost all the consultants interviewed were very much aware of the inherent problems and were concerned that communication between the day hospital and the general practitioner should be effective, particularly concerning drug therapy. The attitude of most consultants was that patients attending day hospitals remained under the care of their general practitioners and that prescribing was therefore the responsibility of the latter. In three day hospitals the patient's medication was left entirely to the general practitioner and in a further nine, although drug treatment might be recommended by staff at the day hospital, it was never prescribed or supplied at the day hospital. In the remaining 18 hospitals, when a change in drug therapy was recommended by the hospital physician, a prescription was given for the first few days' supply and the general practitioner was then asked to give further prescriptions. Eleven of these 18 hospitals simply sent a letter to the general practitioner describing the change in treatment, and seven wrote the change on a treatment card which the patient could subsequently show his general practitioner. The idea of the treatment card—or 'co-operation card' as it was known in one day hospital—was that general practitioners would also record any changes they made in drug treatment and the patient's medication would therefore be clear to both parties at any time. In practice, however, physicians at several of the day hospitals using treatment cards found that they were not kept up to date for some reason, often because patients would forget to take them to their general practitioner or to bring the cards to the day hospital. There seems to be no easy answer to this problem and most of the physicians working in day hospitals found they had to ask patients periodically to bring in all their drugs to find out what they were taking. But this is not foolproof: patients may bring most prescribed drugs but preparations which they have bought over the counter are usually left at home.

Better contact with general practitioners would undoubtedly make for better care for other reasons. In only two of the day hospitals visited did general practitioners attend case conferences: in one of these a small number of local general practitioners in the area had expressed an interest in attending case conferences when one of their patients was being discussed; in the other the general practitioners of all the patients to be discussed at the week's case conference were informed in advance and many attended frequently. The case conference at this day hospital was held at lunch time and any general practitioners who came along were able to discuss their patients with the day hospital staff over a buffet lunch. That more general practitioners might appreciate this kind of involvement in the day hospital is suggested by Hildick-Smith's survey in which 70 per cent of doctors questioned said that they would like to know more about the day hospital.*

Community services

Most day hospital staff regarded their links with the community services as satisfactory. Staff in seven hospitals had some kind of formal meeting with community workers, not necessarily specifically to discuss day hospital patients, but at which the day hospital would be represented. Contact of a more informal kind was maintained by 18 hospitals, but this was felt to be quite satisfactory. In the remaining five, contact with community workers was felt to be inadequate.

There was little difference of opinion between different groups of day hospital staff on this question. All the social workers, as indeed one would hope, were satisfied with their links with the community services and so were all but 8 per cent of the occupational therapists. Twenty-three per cent of physicians and 17 per cent of nurses expressed dissatisfaction, but the most dissatisfied group were the physiotherapists, 27 per cent of whom were unhappy about it.

At most day hospitals requests for local authority residential accommodation, and services such as meals on wheels and home helps, were made by the social workers. Where no social worker was readily available, mainly in the smaller and more isolated hospitals, the sister-in-charge would pass on such requests to the area social workers. The occupational therapists made their own

*See footnote, page 12.

arrangements with social services about providing aids and appliances, and most felt that their job was considerably easier if the local authority had an occupational therapist working in the community. Arrangements for district nursing were always made by the sister-in-charge, and hospitals which had regular contact with the district nursing services had few problems.

The social workers were asked whether they felt that day hospital patients tended to suffer because responsibility for them fell between the community and the hospital-based social workers. Generally, this was not seen as a problem: certainly the social workers were less concerned about this than were the physicians over the similar question of medical supervision of day hospital patients. Many social workers felt that becoming part of the area team had significantly improved their links with their community-based colleagues and that their informal cooperation gave patients a satisfactory service. Two social workers, however, agreed that patients occasionally missed out when the community worker thought that her hospital colleague was looking after the social care, and vice versa.

There was a strong impression, in most of the day hospitals visited, among physicians, nurses and remedial therapists, that many patients were obliged to continue attending the day hospital for maintenance or social care when they could, more appropriately, have started attending a local authority day centre, if a place or transport had been available. Staff in some day hospitals said the waiting time for referral to a day centre could vary from weeks to many months, and some said that places at day centres, even if available in the area, would not be used, usually because of lack of transport. We return to these questions in the last chapter.

Although some day hospitals had a positive policy of discharging patients who would have been more appropriately placed at a day centre, even if there was little chance of a place becoming available, others accepted the responsibility for providing day care in these circumstances for patients not requiring active treatment. In practice it may be difficult to make a clear distinction between the chronically disabled patient who needs day hospital treatment aimed at physical maintenance and the chronically disabled patient who could be adequately managed with social care at a day centre. The remedial therapists will have taught him how best to live with his disability and any nursing required can be adequately provided by the community nurse. In fact, patients attending day hospitals are regarded by many social services departments as requiring too much attention to be suitable for day centre care. Some day centres may have adequate staff to look after significantly disabled patients; many others have not. Further, most local authorities admit to a shortage of day care facilities for the elderly, and although attempts are being made to improve the provision, it has been said that day care has a lower priority than residential care with most social services departments (Matthews 1974).[54]

Joint ventures

It is perhaps not surprising that in some areas an attempt has been made to use the same premises both as a day hospital and as a day centre. The best known of these ventures between the health authority and the local authority is the South Western Day Hospital in St Thomas' Health District, London. This is a large purpose-built day unit which was planned to combine the functions of day centre and day hospital.* The unit incorporates facilities specially for those attending mainly for social reasons, such as a television room, a library and so on, with the active treatment facilities required by day hospital patients. The unit has places for 60 people and transport is provided both by an

*Dr T C Picton Williams has described the unit in detail in a paper, *St Thomas' Hospital geriatric day unit at the South Western Hospital, 1973*, available from the St Thomas' Hospital School of Physiotherapy.

ambulance service based at the day hospital and by social service vehicles. The patients referred from social services go to the geriatric unit and care is taken not to accept those who could equally well attend one of the local authority's other day centres. Suitable referrals are those requiring such attention that the standard day centre would find it difficult to provide. Thus, a day hospital patient who has completed a course of active treatment may continue attending the unit as a social services client; and a client who comes to need the treatment facilities of the unit may become a day hospital patient.

A similar unit has been set up at Lamellion Hospital, Liskeard in the Plymouth Health District. This rural area of Cornwall has virtually no day care facilities provided by the local authority. The local authority pays for each social services client attending the day hospital. It started well as a joint venture, but since the consultant post in the district became vacant, social services clients have tended to predominate in the day hospital and there is less scope for active treatment.

A third similar joint-purpose unit is at St Matthew's Hospital, Tower Hamlets District, where the 60 attendances daily are made up of 20 long-stay inpatients from the hospital who use the unit as a recreation centre, 20 'club members' who use the unit as a day centre and come from their homes either by social services transport or public transport, and 20 day hospital patients who have access to the recreational opportunities of the others but who can also have active treatment as required in the hospital's physiotherapy and occupational therapy departments. The concept and development of this unit are discussed in more detail by the originator, Dr C P Silver.[69]

These examples of cooperation between the local authority and the hospital service were impressive, and indeed went some way towards solving the problem of the patient who no longer needs active treatment at the day hospital but remains too disabled for the usual local authority day centre. The concept of a joint unit has been criticised, however, by Greenfield[33], who suggested that a hospital setting for a social day client might be inhibiting or demoralising, and if patients were to progress to day centres from day hospitals it would be better if this took them outside the hospital confines, to a club or day centre nearer their home. Probably most geriatricians at the present time would agree with Greenfield's view.

It seems that there is scope for experimentation in the relationship between day hospitals and day centres, as is the case in North America at the present time, but there can be little doubt of the need for closer cooperation.

7
Staff's views of their work

Summary

Half of those interviewed felt that the numbers of staff were inadequate—particularly for remedial therapy. This feeling was especially marked among staff working in adapted premises. Nurses tended to see themselves as undertaking duties other than nursing—senior nurses involved in administration, for example—and many would have appreciated a more positive role in rehabilitation. Only 10 per cent were involved in remedial group therapy. Seventy per cent of remedial therapists regarded their essential role as rehabilitation; 30 per cent were positive about the value of maintenance therapy. Sessions of group therapy were organised by 73 per cent of occupational therapists and by 50 per cent of physiotherapists. Both occupational therapists (73 per cent) and physiotherapists (13 per cent) visited patients at home, and one day hospital operated a domiciliary physiotherapy service. None of the social workers interviewed was solely committed to the day hospital, but about half of them regularly attended case conferences. Sixty-six per cent of all staff interviewed thought the team work in their hospitals was good.

Staff

Most of the consultant geriatricians interviewed in the 30 day hospitals visited were asked if recruitment of staff was up to the funded establishment and if they thought that establishment was adequate. The nurses and remedial therapists were also asked about this as it applied to their own departments. Half the staff thought the staffing levels were too low, although only 15 per cent regarded the funded establishment as inadequate. There is some doubt about the accuracy of these data since many members of staff did not know precisely what the funded establishment for the day hospital was. The nurses were, on the whole satisfied, but it seems that recruitment is a serious problem in day hospitals, predominantly in physiotherapy and occupational therapy. The consultants indicated that their major concern was the shortage of remedial therapists, particularly of occupational therapists. There was a difference between the answers to these questions by staff working in purpose-built day hospitals and those working in adapted premises: 37 per cent of staff in the former, but 60 per cent of those in the latter, were dissatisfied.

Nurses

Most of the nurses saw themselves as being something of a 'jack-of-all-trades'. Those in day-to-day charge of the day hospital said that up to half of their time was spent essentially on administrative work, although this was lessened considerably where a clerical officer was responsible for making appointments, arranging transport and so on. Junior nurses were seen as primarily performing nurses' duties in many day hospitals, but many nurses were equivocal about their role in relation to the remedial therapists. Many nurses would like to take a more active role in rehabilitation and to have some training in the techniques used by physiotherapists and occupational therapists. Some said that the nurse in the day hospital should be a 'rehabilitation nurse'.

Eighty per cent of the nurses said that the roles of nurses and remedial staff overlapped and 25 per cent said that this sometimes created problems—often over quite trivial matters such as whether therapists should take patients to the lavatory.

One area of rehabilitation in which nurses could be usefully involved is that of group therapy. However, only 10 per cent of the nurses interviewed in fact organised simple exercises for patients in groups, usually in the smaller day hospitals where remedial therapy time was at a premium.

The nurses tended to be more tolerant of the problems caused by demented and incontinent patients than were the remedial therapists. Most nurses regarded incontinence as in itself a valid reason for patients being referred to the day hospital for assessment and treatment. Fewer thought that dementia was a satisfactory reason for referral and most emphasised that the proportion of demented patients should be kept low. Almost all agreed that it was their job to supervise patients' drug treatment but this was usually confined to supervising specifically a few patients on complex treatment regimes and those who were liable to forget to take their medicines. In only two of the 30 day hospitals was a drug round, comparable with that in an inpatient ward, carried out by a nurse. Most felt that this would be unnecessary.

Nursing notes on patients were usually written in a report book or Kardex. Nursing notes written in the patients' medical folders was the practice in only two hospitals.

Remedial therapists

Generally, physiotherapists and occupational therapists were a good deal more definite about their roles in the day hospital than were the nurses. Most saw themselves as being essentially concerned with rehabilitation, but some (30 per cent) emphasised the importance of maintenance treatment, especially in physiotherapy, in keeping patients out of hospital.

Physiotherapists and occupational therapists usually had a good working relationship and the areas of overlap were not seen as causing any problems. Most were delighted that the day hospital enabled them to work in close proximity. Many had excellent working relationships with the nurses, too. Some were unhappy about the suggestion that nurses should be actively involved in rehabilitation: they agreed that nurses should back up the work of the remedial therapists in encouraging patients to be independent, but not that they should be taught the techniques of physiotherapy and occupational therapy.

Therapists almost universally considered that only fairly basic apparatus was necessary for their work with the elderly. Physiotherapists felt that provided they had plinths, parallel bars, simple exercise apparatus, such as springs and pulleys and exercise bicycles or rowing machines, and enough different walking aids and wheelchairs, they could cope with most of the problems presented by the patients. More complex apparatus was seen as unnecessary, and most therapists said that they spent relatively little time giving physical treatment to patients. Equipment such as wax baths, shortwave diathermy and so on was regarded as a luxury in the day hospital. Many therapists felt that it was inappropriate to spend their relatively limited time with patients giving palliative heat treatment for conditions such as osteoarthrosis, when the basic need was to teach patients to live as independently as possible within the limitations of their disability.

Occupational therapists had similar views. For example, the kitchens and bedrooms for assessing disability should not be oversupplied with complex apparatus designed for the disabled, since it was often difficult to teach elderly patients to use it, and the chances of being able to provide it at home were small.

Thus, while occupational therapists needed a supply of simple, 'one-handed' gadgets—such as wall can-openers, bread boards with a stop at the end and vegetable boards spiked to allow one-handed peeling—there would be little point in having a full 'wheelchair kitchen', or beds and chairs with electrically operated raising devices.

Seventy-three per cent of the occupational therapists and 50 per cent of the physiotherapists used group therapy techniques. Quite often, groups were supervised by the qualified therapist but the sessions were taken by an aide. Most therapists preferred qualified remedial staff to be involved in groups and many were doubtful about group therapy arranged by nurses. In only six of the 30 day hospitals were there no group therapy sessions involving remedial therapists. In three hospitals, remedial staff were so scarce that only group therapy could be offered. These were hospitals with a low turnover of patients and an emphasis on maintenance and social care rather than on active treatment.

Sixty-seven per cent of occupational therapists visited patients at home for assessment. The remainder generally did not have enough time and were obliged to rely either on their colleagues in the area for assessment or on other community workers where there were no area occupational therapists. In one or two instances, the occupational therapists said that they were not allowed to do assessment visits.

We were surprised to find that only a small proportion of physiotherapists (13 per cent) visited patients at home. This was generally regarded as inappropriate for physiotherapists, home assessment being the role of the occupational therapist. In only three day hospitals did physiotherapists and occupational therapists go out together for domiciliary assessments; in two of these a nurse sometimes accompanied the therapists and was thought to make a useful contribution to the assessment. Nurses gave the impression that they would have liked more opportunity to visit patients at home but most remedial therapists thought the presence of a nurse on a home visit was quite unnecessary.

Only one day hospital had a domiciliary physiotherapy service, although in three units there was a domiciliary service operating from the main hospital physiotherapy department. Many physiotherapists said they would like to see the development of a domiciliary service operating from the day hospital; it would cater for those patients not needing inpatient admission but too disabled to come to the day hospital. It could, of course, also cater for patients awaiting admission and might well be a much more effective way of training relatives in the techniques of managing disabled patients. Therapists on the whole were happy to welcome relatives to the day hospital, generally by appointment, to discuss their individual problems but most tended to wait for relatives to approach them rather than making the approach themselves.

Like the nurses, remedial therapists tended to have their own notes about patients rather than write in the medical notes, and generally they seemed to prefer this system.

Social workers

None of the social workers interviewed was solely committed to the day hospital and most only visited on demand. Many would have liked to devote more time to day hospital patients rather than leaving them to their community-based colleagues. Only 35 per cent regularly attended case conferences, but this is not a representative picture since at 16 day hospitals no social worker was available for interview; at eight of these we were informed by other members of staff that social workers usually attended case conferences.

In two units where a social worker saw a new client—that is, one previously unknown to the social services—she would follow up that patient on discharge and a community-based social worker would not be involved. At the same time community-based social workers would follow up clients known to them when they were admitted to hospital without necessarily involving the hospital-based social worker. This system was said to have many advantages—notably avoiding duplication of work—although occasionally it was a problem to find out which social worker a patient had seen in the past and this caused delay.

Social workers were generally reluctant to comment about the running of the day hospital since their involvement was limited, but most felt that it was very useful to them in their work, particularly where the provision of day care by the social services was inadequate. One hospital we visited stayed open during the weekend and the social worker here thought this was essential because the community social services provided limited care at this time.

Other staff

No speech therapists, chiropodists, opticians or other staff who gave occasional sessions to the day hospital were formally interviewed, but several were seen briefly during our visits, and almost all saw the day hospital as very useful and an excellent way of caring for patients not requiring admission to hospital. Facilities for chiropodists were poor; a room set aside solely for chiropody was unusual.

Some day hospitals had craft teachers employed by the local authority and a few had voluntary workers. Where these groups were involved in the day hospital, the other staff felt that they were very helpful and useful colleagues.

Team work

Perhaps the most important question is whether the staff work together satisfactorily as a team. Altogether, 66 per cent of the staff interviewed considered that the team feeling was strong and that all staff worked together well. Seventeen per cent, however, thought that they were working too much in isolation; these were predominantly physiotherapists (33 per cent of that group) and occupational therapists (29 per cent).

Four per cent of staff, nearly all of them nurses, regarded their roles as insufficiently defined.

In all, 13 per cent of staff were somewhat equivocal about team work and felt that there was some lack of understanding of each other's roles. They tended to be staff in the day hospitals where there was relatively little contact between the physicians, nurses and therapists.

Again we found some differences between staff working in adapted premises and those in purpose-built day hospitals. In the adapted units, 57 per cent of staff were satisfied with the team work and 25 per cent felt that staff worked too much in isolation—this was very often a physical isolation brought about by the nature of the premises. In the purpose-built day hospitals, on the other hand, 75 per cent of staff were satisfied with the team work and only 10 per cent felt that they worked too much in isolation from the others.

The majority of staff, then, were enthusiastic about team work. Personality clashes, leading to some degree of isolationism, did not seem to be at all widespread. Difficulties arose more from the unsuitability of the premises rather than from any lack of good will.

8

Patients and their relatives

Summary

Details of 233 patients attending 30 day hospitals were obtained. Just over half the staff interviewed thought that most referrals were appropriate; 19 per cent, mainly remedial therapists, thought there was a high proportion of inappropriate referrals. The most common principal diagnoses were stroke (37 per cent) and arthritis (22 per cent); the least common were dementia (4 per cent) and depression (3 per cent). Social problems, usually that of living alone, were present in 28 per cent. The main reasons for attendance, as seen by the staff, were rehabilitation (43 per cent) and maintenance (21 per cent), but sometimes staff did not know why patients were attending. More than half the patients had been attending for up to six months; a quarter for over a year. Length of attendance varied according to the reason for attendance. Eighty per cent received occupational therapy and 62 per cent physiotherapy. In some hospitals, each patient was given a 'package' therapy regardless of diagnosis or reason for attendance.

Interviews were undertaken with 173 patients and 74 relatives. Nearly all the patients (93 per cent) enjoyed the social aspects of day hospital care, 64 per cent thought the therapeutic programme did them good, and 44 per cent said they had improved. Half the relatives thought the social and psychological benefits were the most obvious and a third saw improvement in their patients' physical condition. Three-quarters of the relatives saw the major benefit to them as the temporary freedom the day hospital gave. Most patients came by ambulance, which was part of the enjoyment, and though some complained of timing none complained of the ambulance staff. Most patients, but only a third of their relatives, thought they had enough to occupy their time at the day hospital.

It was not always clear who cared for the patient at home; the staff sometimes did not identify the same person as did the patients. In half the cases, where the staff thought no one in particular was looking after the patient at home, the patient himself identified someone. We recommend that this information should be recorded in the patients' case notes.

Who attends the day hospital? With whom do they live, and who looks after them at home? What is their principal diagnosis? Why are they attending the day hospital? How long have they been attending? What treatment are they receiving? And what do they think about it all?

To try to answer these questions a random sample of eight patients in each of the 30 day hospitals visited was selected. The total number attending on the day of our visit was divided by eight and that number used for selecting patients from the attendance register. In two day hospitals, only six patients were attending on the day and therefore available for interview. Information about the patients was obtained from the sister-in-charge, in association with the other members of the staff.

The information is complete in 233 of the 236 patients selected. The remaining three were attending dual-purpose day hospitals as day centre cases. On a second visit the research assistant personally interviewed 178 of these patients. The others were not interviewed either because there was no time or because the patients could not be found.

The age range of the patients was as follows.

	%
Under 65	5
65 - 75	40
76 - 85	42
over 85	13

Sixty-three patients were men and 170 were women.

Medical and social problems

As expected, a large number of patients had more than one diagnosis. The major diagnostic categories, as perceived by the day hospital staff and recorded in the patients' notes, are shown in Table 13. In no case were more than three diagnoses recorded. The commonest primary diagnosis was stroke (37 per cent), followed by joint disease (22 per cent), osteoarthrosis being much commoner than rheumatoid arthritis. 'Other' diagnoses included diabetes, hypertension, anaemia and ischaemic heart disease. Eleven patients had undiagnosed problems—falls, postural instability and 'old age'.

Comments were also invited from the sister-in-charge on problems other than medical, and were recorded in 66 patients. Living alone was the most frequent problem (40 patients). Other problems mentioned were poor conditions at home (4), tension between patient and relatives (4) or overprotection by relatives (4). One patient was thought to be neglecting himself, two had been

Table 13 Diagnoses of 233 patients

	primary	*secondary*	*tertiary*
stroke	86 (37%)	6	1
arthritis	51 (22%)	7	1
parkinsonism	11 (4.5%)	5	–
amputation	10 (4%)	–	–
paraplegia	9 (4%)	–	–
dementia	9 (4%)	12	2
depression	8 (3.5%)	9	1
respiratory	7 (3%)	4	1
leg ulcer	6 (2.5%)	9	1
femoral neck fracture	2 (1%)	4	1
incontinence	2 (1%)	8	2
other	21 (9%)	55	11
undiagnosed	11 (4.5%)	6	2

recently bereaved and two were living in lodging houses. Ten patients were referred to simply as having or perhaps being, a social problem. A more detailed profile of the social background of many of these patients would have been known to the social worker, but was often not recorded in the medical notes.

Reason for attendance

The principal diagnosis recorded in the case notes does not indicate why the patient is attending the day hospital. For instance, a patient with stroke may be attending for rehabilitation, physical maintenance, to give a daughter a break, to overcome loneliness, for the management of associated incontinence, or for several of these and other reasons. The day hospital sister was therefore asked to specify the reason for each patient's attendance. Of the 233 patients, 93 were said to be coming to the day hospital for more than one reason and seven patients had three reasons for attendance. Rehabilitation was the primary reason most frequently given (see Table 14).

Table 14 Reasons for attendance of 233 patients

	primary	*secondary*	*third*
rehabilitation	99 (42.5%)	4	–
maintenance	48 (20.5%)	10	1
medical supervision	30 (13%)	17	2
nursing procedures	14 (6%)	13	3
social	31 (13%)	36	1
relatives' relief	8 (3.5%)	13	–
not known	3 (1.5%)	–	–

These figures may be compared with those for 465 patients surveyed by Brocklehurst in 1970.[12]

	%
rehabilitation	27
physical maintenance	42
social reasons	26
other	5

Reasons for attendance then and in the present survey show marked differences–particularly for two categories, rehabilitation and maintenance.

Table 15 Duration of attendance compared with reasons for attendance

	months				*years*			
	up to 1 %	*1–3* %	*3–6* %	*6–12* %	*1–3* %	*3 or more* %	*not known* %	*total numbers*
rehabilitation	29	23	18	16	9	3	2	99
maintenance	13	6	10	21	23	27	–	48
medical supervision	23	17	23	27	10	–	–	30
nursing procedures	8	29	21	21	14	7	–	14
social	16	10	20	23	26	5	–	31
relatives' relief	13	24	13	13	24	13	–	8
not known	–	100	–	–	–	–	–	3
total	21	18	17	19	15	9	1	233

However, staff often had difficulty in defining the reasons for attendance. In many instances it was only after considerable thought that a patient was put in the category of rehabilitation or of maintenance, and often discussion with other members of staff was necessary before an answer could be reached. Sometimes the reason for attendance had changed according to the patient's progress or lack of it; and sometimes it was difficult to decide which was the primary and which the secondary reason. Staff had most difficulty in placing the patients who had been attending for many months or years, and this emphasises the importance of a regular multidisciplinary review of patients.

The length of time each patient had been attending the day hospital varied enormously, the longest unbroken period being six and a half years. Many patients had had more than one period of attendance but only the duration of the current attendance was recorded. Table 15 compares this with the reasons for attendance. It will be seen that 39 per cent had attended for up to three months, 17 per cent between three and six months, and 43 per cent for longer. The figures show that a somewhat shorter period of attendance is more usual now than in Brocklehurst's earlier survey, which showed that 30 per cent had attended for less than three months, and 53 per cent for longer than six months.

As might be expected, more patients attending for rehabilitation had been coming for relatively short periods but some of those attending for six months or longer would probably have been more appropriately placed as attending for physical maintenance. Most of them were stroke patients in whom it might be expected that the maximum potential for recovery would be reached by six months.

Treatment

The staff were asked to state the treatment which each patient received, and we have compared this in Table 16 with the reason for attendance, and in Table 17 with the primary diagnosis. It should be noted that information was not obtained on whether remedial therapy was given individually or in groups, or whether it was specific or general. We imply, however, that activities under the headings 'occupational therapy' and 'physiotherapy' cover a wide range.

It will be seen that the proportion of patients receiving occupational therapy is high, whatever the reason for attendance, while the proportion receiving physiotherapy is a good deal lower in the patients attending primarily for medical supervision, nursing procedures and social reasons. Many of those whose primary reason for attendance was relief of relatives were receiving occupational therapy and physiotherapy, but the total number of such patients was fairly small.

Table 16 Reason for attendance compared with treatment received

	occupational therapy %	*physio-therapy* %	*speech therapy* %	*chiropody* %	*bath* %	*special nursing* %
rehabilitation n = 99	92	87	15	19	27	29
maintenance n = 48	81	79	–	13	35	15
medical supervision n = 30	57	43	–	7	13	17
nursing procedures n = 14	71	43	–	21	29	93
social n = 31	65	32	3	13	29	10
relatives' relief n = 8	88	75	–	25	38	25
not known n = 3	75	75	33	–	–	75
total % n = 233	80	69	7	16	28	26

The number of baths given varied considerably. At some day hospitals regular baths were given to all patients; in others they were offered only exceptionally. Under the heading 'special nursing' we have included catheter care, enemata, injections and dressings.

From our interviews with staff it appeared that many day hospitals were offering the same 'package' of treatment to patients regard-

Table 17 Treatment received compared with primary diagnosis

	occupational therapy %	*physio-therapy* %	*speech therapy* %	*chiropody* %	*bath* %	*special nursing* %
stroke n = 86	94	87	17	21	27	23
arthritis n = 51	80	84	–	12	31	19
parkinsonism n = 11	73	73	9	9	18	36
amputation n = 10	70	90	–	20	30	40
paraplegia n = 9	56	33	–	11	44	22
dementia n = 9	100	33	–	11	44	44
depression n = 8	100	38	–	25	25	–
respiratory n = 7	57	28	–	–	14	29
leg ulcer n = 6	100	50	–	33	17	83
femoral neck fracture n = 2	50	50	–	–	–	50
incontinence n = 2	50	50	–	50	50	50
other n = 21	48	24	–	9	19	14
undiagnosed n = 11	55	55	–	9	18	27

less of the individual diagnosis or reason for attendance. There seemed to be a need for more precise programming of each patient's treatment (possibly by a multidisciplinary committee of staff). Some patients were almost certainly having unnecessary or unproductive remedial therapy, and this was borne out in conversation with therapists at several hospitals.

The chief carer

Where a patient was living with his or her next of kin, information about the person chiefly concerned with his care at home was readily available from the medical notes. Often, however, although the name of the next of kin was known, the person actually looking after the patient was not recorded and was difficult to ascertain. When the patients were asked 'Who looks after you?', the answer did not always agree with the staff's perception, particularly when they believed that no one looked after the patient. In half these cases, the patient quoted someone—a relative, neighbour or, occasionally, home help—as the chief carer. Table 18 shows who, according to the staff, looked after the patient at home. Of these 228 patients, 174 were subsequently interviewed by the research assistant and 36 (21 per cent) disagreed with the answer given by the day hospital staff, usually when the person chiefly concerned with his care did not live with the patient.

In some day hospitals the chief carers were well known, but in many the questions were answered only with difficulty. In many smaller day hospitals each patient was known to the sister, and the details, whilst not always recorded, were familiar to her. In the larger day hospitals the details in some cases were neither known nor recorded, and had to be ascertained during our interviews. This appears to be basic information which should be readily available and recorded in a patient's medical record. Much of it could be included in a master problem list at the front of the case notes.

Table 18 Chief carers

		living with patient
daughter (with son-in-law)	49 (21%)	21
husband	36 (16%)	36
son (with daughter-in-law)	35 (15%)	18
wife	30 (13%)	30
sister	12 (5%)	6
matron of home	8 (4%)	7
warden of flats	8 (4%)	1
brother	6 (3%)	2
other relative	5 (2%)	1
neighbour	4 (2%)	–
friend	4 (2%)	2
landlord	3 (1%)	–
home help	3 (1%)	–
no one	25 (11%)	–

Appropriateness of referral

The question of how many of the patients attending day hospitals are appropriately placed is very important. At each hospital, the staff were asked if they considered referrals on the whole to be appropriate for a day hospital. Over all, 53 per cent felt that the great majority of referrals were appopriate; but 28 per cent felt that, whilst many referrals were appropriate, some patients should not have been attending a day hospital, and the remaining 19 per cent felt that a high proportion of referrals was unsuitable. Physiotherapists and occupational therapists were most likely to feel that patients were inappropriately placed, and many thought that patients who were not capable of being rehabilitated were being referred to them for treatment when they should have been receiving care in a social day centre. Therapists had very mixed views about maintenance therapy for such patients: some were enthusiastic, others singularly unconvinced of its value.

By no means all the consultants were happy that all the patients referred to the day hospital should have been attending. Several said that if day care facilities provided by social services had been better, the demand for attendance at day hospitals would be less.

The social workers (86 per cent) and the nurses (70 per cent) were most likely to feel that the majority of referrals were appropriate.

The patients' views

There have been relatively few attempts to determine patients' views about day hospital treatment. Peach and Pathy (1977), using the technique of linear analogue self-assessment, reported the views of 51 patients about their journey to the day hospital, how enjoyable and helpful the time spent at the day hospital had been, how useful the time spent with doctors, nurses and remedial therapists had been, and whether the patients would be prepared to attend the day hospital again if the need arose. Patients were found to be generally appreciative of their treatment, and most were keen to attend again if necessary.[60]

Our research assistant interviewed 174 patients, only one of whom refused to answer any questions.

Fifty-six per cent of the patients lived in houses, 29 per cent in flats, 9 per cent in bungalows and 6 per cent in nursing homes, old people's homes or other accommodation such as lodging houses.

An attempt was made to ascertain the social class of each patient by asking the men and single women, 'What was your job before retiring?', and the married women and widows, 'What is (or was) your husband's job?'. Findings, coded according to the Office of Population Censuses and Surveys, Classification of Occupations, 1970 (appendix B1)* showed a predominance of skilled manual and non-manual workers (47 per cent) in exactly the same proportion as the general population. Of the remainder, 17 per cent were social classes I and II, compared with 25 per cent in the general population, and 36 per cent in social classes IV and V compared with 27 per cent in the general population.

Thirty-seven per cent of patients lived alone, 28 per cent with a spouse and 21 per cent with a son or daughter (married or single). Four per cent lived with a brother or sister, and the remaining 10 per cent lived with friends, had a landlord living in the same premises or were residents in old people's homes. The number of single-person households (37 per cent) may be compared with that in the Age Concern survey (Abrams, 1978) which showed 33 per cent of all those aged 65 and over, and 47 per cent of those aged 75 and over, were living alone.[1] By this comparison, the number of day hospital attenders in these age groups is not excessive, and this suggests that isolation is not in itself seen as a reason for attendance at a day hospital. The Age Concern survey showed that membership of clubs for the elderly was higher among those living alone than others, but even here the figures were not high; over 80 per cent of those living alone did not belong to clubs.

In response to the question, 'Who looks after you?', all 49 patients (28 per cent) who had a living spouse replied that he or she was the chief carer. Forty-two per cent were looked after by their children but these were not necessarily living with the patients.

*The Registrar General in Great Britain designates the social classes according to occupation as follows: I and II, professional and managerial; III, skilled manual workers; IV and V, unskilled manual workers.

Six per cent were looked after by a brother or sister—again, not necessarily living with the patient. The views of these relatives are described later in this chapter.

Nearly all the patients (84 per cent) came to the day hospital by ambulance, 13 per cent by private cars (either driven by relatives or in hospital cars) and 3 per cent by other means, such as in a minibus run by the day hospital. Those who came by ambulance were asked what time it called that morning. The most usual time seemed to be between 8.30 and 9.30am (54 per cent). Only 2 per cent were collected before 8.30am, 26 per cent between 9.30 and 10.00am and 18 per cent after 10.00am. Since complaints of ambulances arriving very late are often heard in day hospitals, it is surprising that more patients were not collected later than 10.00am.

The impression that patients often rise very early in order to be in time for the ambulance was certainly borne out by the answers to the question, 'What time did you get up this morning?'. No less than 51 per cent of patients had risen before 7.00am, including 17 per cent who had risen before 6.00am. Approximately half the patients said they usually got up at that time. If these patients are representative of the elderly as a whole, there is still a large number of early risers amongst them. When asked if the ambulance usually came on time, 47 per cent replied that it did and 53 per cent that it did not.

Most patients (88 per cent) enjoyed the ambulance ride, while 11 per cent said that they did not and 1 per cent did not know. Those who enjoyed the ride were asked why. A third of them referred to the convenience of coming by ambulance (in many cases linking with this their disabilities), 27 per cent mentioned the helpfulness of staff and 20 per cent found the journey itself a pleasant part of the day. A further 13 per cent gave all these reasons. A few patients gave non-specific answers, *'It's the only way to come'* or *'It's all right'*, or stated that they enjoyed the company of other passengers.

Those patients who had answered 'No' to the question about the ambulance ride were also asked why. Their replies were about the journey itself—that it was uncomfortable, too long or boring. None of them criticised the ambulance staff.

A very high percentage, 93 per cent, enjoyed attending the day hospital; only 5 per cent did not and 2 per cent did not know. The social aspects of day hospital care were the ones which patients enjoyed most: 67 per cent of the replies were concerned with these, 19 per cent of patients specifically mentioned that they liked the staff and found them helpful, 28 per cent the company of the other patients and 8 per cent the entertainments and games or the midday meal. For 12 per cent it was a mixture of these, mainly the staff and the company of other patients. Seventeen per cent gave replies suggesting that they liked both the treatment and social aspects of day hospital care and 12 per cent said that they liked the medical or remedial treatment. There were a few non-specific replies such as *'It's all right'*.

> *I like the homely atmosphere—it doesn't seem like a hospital.*

> *It gives me a big lift—if you were just in the house all the time you might as well be in prison.*

> *I've felt different since I have been coming here. I am now having care and attention and they bath me when I come. I shall be worried when they have to discharge me.*

> *It has been a great help in readjusting to life since my husband's death.*

Patients were also asked, 'What don't you like about the day hospital?', and 29 (17 per cent) commented on this though most of them said that over all they enjoyed attending. Seven patients did not enjoy their medical or remedial therapy, and six patients complained that they had to wait around too long either because of unpredictable transport or because there was not enough to do in the day hospital. Three patients did not enjoy mixing with the other patients and five patients said that they were upset by seeing sick people. Three patients said that they simply did not like the idea of coming to a hospital.

> *I don't like leaving my own home for the day because I don't have many years left to live.*

> *I don't like to see people falling, people ill. The day drags, and it seems rather a long time to be here.*

> *I think we have too many childish games. I wish the occupational therapy was more advanced here. They need more staff and it would be helpful if they could find more ways to make patients keep their brains active, relieving the monotony from dinner time until 3 o'clock.*

Most patients (64 per cent) thought that medical, nursing or remedial treatment was the most important reason for attending the day hospital. Ten per cent felt that a combination of formal treatment and the social aspects was the important thing. Fourteen per cent felt that the social opportunities in the day hospital were the most important part of their treatment. These included meals, being with other people and engaging in activities. A few patients gave non-specific replies, such as *'It's all right'.* Nine per cent seemed unable to give an answer to this question, and 3 per cent could see no reason for coming and said they received no treatment.

When we analysed further the responses citing medical or remedial therapy as the most important part of the treatment, we saw that the vast majority of these 110 patients were referring to physiotherapy and occupational therapy. Five patients referred generally to occupational therapy and 33 to physiotherapy. But 53 patients were more specific: 38 of them said their exercises were the most important part of treatment and 15 mentioned physical treatments, such as wax baths and shortwave diathermy. Only six patients referred to medical advice (with prescriptions for drugs), and only eight to nursing procedures, such as dressings and catheter care, as the most important treatment. Six patients gave mixed or non-specific 'medical' responses to this question.

There was a similar pattern in the patients' views on the benefit of attending the day hospital: 44 thought their condition had improved in a physical sense and most of the replies suggested that this was because of remedial therapy; 39 per cent, however, felt that the social outlet had been most beneficial, 7 per cent that they had benefited both medically and socially, and the remainder were non-specific.

Patients were asked if they had enough to do at the day hospital. Nearly all (87 per cent) said they had. Most of the 11 per cent who felt they had too little to do seemed to feel that they did not have enough individual remedial therapy. Patients were also asked, 'Is there anything you think you have too much of at the day hospital?'. Ten per cent thought there was too much sitting around. One or two patients felt they had too many exercises or too much treatment, and one patient said that there was too much bingo!

Very few patients had any suggestions for improving the day hospital. Nine patients suggested minor improvements in facilities, such as book cases and tables with no sharp edges. Seven patients said that more therapy was required and that the day hospital should have more staff to achieve this. A few patients thought that improvement in transport would improve the day hospital considerably. One patient said, *'I would like to be able to pay something towards the lunches and tea. I would feel more independent.'*

Patients were asked how often they came to the day hospital, and twice weekly seemed to be the commonest pattern. The mean attendance was 1.93 times per week per patient. Finally, patients were asked if they went out on the days they did not attend the day hospital. It is perhaps surprising that half of them did: 13 per cent went to a day centre or club; 46 per cent visited friends or relatives or went to church, shops, libraries, pubs, the bank or for car rides and for walks.

It is difficult to know to what extent the patients' true feelings were expressed in these interviews. The elderly are notoriously reluctant to criticise facilities provided for them, and answers such as *'It's not for me to say'* in reply to the question, 'Have you any suggestions to make for improving the day hospital?' bear this out. Replies were probably also influenced by the personality of the interviewer, and the fact that the interview was conducted at the day hospital.

Relatives' views

The research assistant also interviewed 74 relatives of some of the patients. Their relationships were

husband or wife	38
son or daughter	26
brother or sister	7
niece	1

The friend who lived with one of the patients and the matron of a nursing home where another patient lived were also interviewed. For convenience, however, we shall regard these two as relatives of the patient.

They were first asked about transport services. As we have noted, 84 per cent of the patients travelled by ambulance; 13 per cent by private car and 3 per cent by other means, usually minibus. Fifty-seven relatives thought the transport was satisfactory, eleven did not. Six relatives did not know, or the question was not applicable since the patient was driven to the day hospital by the relative.

Of the 57 relatives who approved of the transport service, 48 were able to specify why: 15 referred to the convenience of having the ambulance (or hospital car) call for the patient and four praised the prompt timing; 27 spoke of the helpfulness of the ambulance staff—they were kind and considerate, and one relative commented that the ambulance came back if the patient was not ready. Six replies were non-committal, including comments such as, *'It's the only way to come to the day hospital'.*

Those who were dissatisfied, including five who had stated that the service was satisfactory but qualified this later by pointing out the disadvantages, referred to the unpredictability of the service and that there was too much waiting around for the ambulance to arrive. Five relatives mentioned that the journey was uncomfortable for the patient; two said it made the patient sick. No one referred to unduly long journeys and no one had any criticism of the ambulance staff.

Asked if the patient sometimes had to wait a long time for the ambulance to arrive, 36 said 'No', and 26 said 'Yes, quite often'. Nine said that there was only occasionally a long wait; the remainder did not know.

> *She isn't a good traveller and the ambulance journey is so roundabout and always stopping and starting. Often she is sick when she arrives back in the evening and she can't eat her tea.*

> *He gets fed up waiting for the ambulance and he often refuses to go when they do come—it's so very late.*

The time varies so much when she is brought home—it can be between half past three and half past seven at night. Also, they often cancel the ambulance and this is counterproductive to the whole idea of day hospital.

There is less association with illness travelling in a car.

Relatives were also asked whether day hospital attendance had provided any benefit for the patient: 60 said it had and only four said it had not; 10 did not know. Nineteen relatives thought the benefit had been the improvement in the patient's physical condition, but the largest number of relatives (27), spoke of the social or psychological benefit, and 13 said they saw both physical and social or psychological benefit. One relative thought the main benefit was that the patient was able to get a bath, and another that the patient was losing weight.

There were nine replies to the question 'If there hasn't been a benefit please explain', including those of relatives who qualified their comments about the benefits by pointing out the drawbacks. Some of the 'don't knows' also replied to this question. Six of the nine respondents simply said that there was no benefit, or that none had been expected. Two criticised the treatment the patient was receiving and one criticised the reduced attendance at the day hospital *'just as things were beginning to improve'*.

Relatives were then asked whether it had made any difference to them personally that the patient was attending the day hospital: 58 said that it had and all but four specified the difference. Twenty-one cited the opportunity to go out, do shopping or get on with the housework; 24 said that it was a relief from the worry or strain of looking after the patient or that it gave them a chance to rest. Six relatives gave both these reasons. Only two said that the patient now required less care at home. One relative said that the patient's day hospital attendance was just *'one extra worry'*. It is perhaps disappointing that more relatives did not feel that an improvement in the patient's condition, necessitating less nursing for them, was a major benefit.

Six relatives, however, felt the patient did not seem to be receiving enough treatment. One said *'I only wish she could have more exercises. She does seem to be so much better on the days when she has them.'*

Most of them qualified the statement by saying that they felt there were not enough staff, particularly remedial staff, to give each patient individual treatment. Four respondents said that the main snag was the poor transport service and two blamed the long ambulance journeys for the patients having been incontinent by the time they returned home. Two others complained of poor communication between the day hospital and patients' relatives; they wanted to know much more about the treatment the patient was receiving so that they could help him more effectively at home. Two relatives said that patients were bored at the day hospital and needed more opportunities for diversional work between treatment sessions.

> *My wife doesn't like it. She is not busy enough—she just sits around across from others who don't talk at all. There just isn't enough to occupy her time.*

Another two thought the patient ought to have been able to continue attending the day hospital more frequently; the number of attendances each week had been cut recently in both cases. One relative complained that the patient had not been given a bath although this had been promised and that the day hospital was too noisy.

Relatives were also asked for comments or suggestions about the day hospital. Forty-three relatives replied to this question, and the most frequent suggestion, made by 11 respondents, was that there should be better communication between the day hospital staff and patients' relatives.

I wish they would tell me what is happening. To me I think she has deteriorated, and I think our local GP would confirm this.

I don't really know what they are doing. It would be better if there were some communication between the day hospital and ourselves.

I wish the therapists would now and again send a message through the wife saying how I could help her at home.

Seven respondents said that they felt the day hospital needed more staff to give patients individual treatment. Two thought that the staff should be sympathetic towards providing relief for relatives from caring for the patient at home. Altogether 25 replies were critical and suggested improvements; 14 relatives simply praised the day hospital or the staff.

Staff are very kind and helpful.

She'd be in a home but for the day hospital.

One relative thought that it should be possible for her to contribute to the cost of day hospital care and suggested a box for donations in a prominent place there.

The most interesting point to emerge was that the relatives seemed to know very little about the treatment which the patient was receiving. Many knew very little about the day hospital at all, apart from what the patient was able to tell them. Few relatives had actually visited the day hospital.

I have never been there so I don't know.

This lack of communication between the day hospital and the relatives may underlie many of the patients' problems. For example, to what extent are relatives expected to assist in the programme of rehabilitation started at the day hospital on the days when the patient is at home? Perhaps relatives rely solely on the day hospital for rehabilitation. Further, when the patient is discharged, are relatives involved in any way in continuing rehabilitation and maintenance? One wonders if the staff of day hospitals fully appreciate the role which the relative or family play in helping to maintain patients in the community after discharge or even while attending the day hospital. Lack of communication might be overcome by meetings between relatives and day hospital staff like those we found at the Windsor Day Hospital, Falkirk.

9

Transport

Summary

The day hospital staff saw transport as the biggest problem in day hospital care: half of all those interviewed complained of the unpredictability and 16 per cent thought the journey was too long. In only two day hospitals did the staff agree that were no transport problems. Of the 59 drivers interviewed, 41 used multipurpose vehicles, 10 used sitting-type vehicles, six had minibuses and two used cars. Their main complaints about multipurpose vehicles were poor access and lack of a tail-lift (only 29 per cent of the vehicles had these). Sitting-type ambulances, minibuses and cars were considered most suitable for patients. Most drivers began collecting patients between 8.30 and 9.00am; 11 began before 8.30 and nine after 9.00am. The main problem about collecting patients was that they were often not ready. Twelve drivers had problems about exchanging information with the day hospital. About half the drivers liked working with the day hospital, the others did not. Fourteen drivers said they were often directed to other work when they were scheduled for the day hospital; only 16 said this never happened.

Many drivers thought the day hospital was more a social club than a treatment centre. This may be why the ambulance service gives low priority to day hospital care. The question requires further investigation.

When asked what was their biggest problem, most staff concerned with day hospitals—whether doctors, nurses or remedial therapists—replied ‘transport’. In only two of the 30 day hospitals visited did all the staff agree that there were no transport problems whatsoever: one was the South Western Day Hospital in St Thomas’ Health District, London, where an ambulance had been supplied at the outset and was controlled entirely by the day hospital; the other was Pine Heath Day Hospital in the Norwich Health District where all patients were brought in by car.

Generally, the degree of satisfaction with the transport service was related to the control which the day hospital had over it. Where one or more ambulances were used solely for day hospital patients, the service was usually said to be good; where day hospital patients were ‘fitted in’ with outpatients, and sometimes emergencies as well, the day hospital staff were usually dissatisfied with the service.

Only 15 per cent of all staff interviewed were entirely satisfied; 50 per cent stated that it was too unpredictable or that patients arrived too late and/or departed too early, and 16 per cent felt that the ambulance journeys were too long. The remainder had criticisms—not enough places for patients in the vehicles being used, too many patients were picked up on each run and the vehicle was therefore too crowded, or that patients were often picked up too late in the evening.

The most frequent criticisms concerned timing. Day hospitals want their patients to come at the same time as do outpatient clinics; and the time the day patients need to go home coincides with the time outpatients are returning home from afternoon clinics. These conflicting demands can only be satisfied if transport for the day hospital and for outpatients can be separated, so that some vehicles are used only for day hospital patients during the peak periods. It is usually, however, unacceptable to have ambulances standing idle from mid-morning to mid-afternoon and difficult to use them for other purposes only at these times.

How early can patients reasonably be picked up in the morning? Ambulance drivers' shifts and consideration for patients demand that it should not generally be before 8.30am and, with journey times of an hour or more, few patients will arrive at the day hospital before 10.00am. Staff were usually happy to have patients arriving between 10.00 and 11.00am, but thought that later arrival was unacceptable, especially if the journey home had to start at 3.00pm, or earlier. Late departure, though a less common problem, caused a great deal of worry to patients. Staff at three day hospitals reported that patients sometimes waited up to 7.00pm before the ambulance arrived to take them home, and occasionally even later. The worst transport 'horror story' we heard concerned a patient who had waited so long for her ambulance that it had been decided to put her to bed in one of the wards. When the ambulance eventually arrived, the ambulancemen got her up out of bed and took her home at around 10.30pm!

Long journeys are another problem, especially when very large vehicles are used. We have noted that many patients seem to enjoy the journey to the day hospital, but others find it uncomfortable. The circuitous journey picking up patients at many points has been criticised by several authors, including Hildick-Smith[38] and Arie.[4] The latter, perhaps with tongue in cheek, suggested that as the problem is so common we should consider using it as a form of therapy. 'Transport therapy' would consist of jogging the patient along in the ambulance for several hours with a break at a transport cafe!

Transport poses a particular problem in the country where the day hospital may have a very large catchment area. Some of the rural day hospitals limited their facilities to patients who lived within 10 miles; others had no fixed limit, but most patients in fact lived within 10 miles or so of the day hospital. We found that one patient lived 20 miles away. Probably general practitioners a long way from a day hospital would tend not to refer patients for treatment. Hildick-Smith found that a high proportion of the general practitioners who never referred patients to a day hospital practised more than 10 miles from the nearest one.

Despite their criticisms of the service, most of the day hospital staff paid tribute to the drivers' concern for their patients, and many stated that the 'information service' provided by drivers on the patients' homes was very useful.

Vehicles used

A multipurpose vehicle is one used for both emergency and non-emergency cases. It has stretchers which, with the use of seat belts, can become seats for patients who can walk with assistance. It may also have chairs, but most multipurpose vehicles have stretchers on either side of the interior.

A sitting-type vehicle has chairs fixed in the ambulance itself and is therefore available only for patients attending day hospitals or outpatient departments. Such vehicles are usually operated by one man and for this reason patients must be fairly mobile.

Other vehicles used included ordinary cars—sometimes private cars driven by relatives and sometimes hospital cars—and minibuses, usually used only for the day hospital, and usually larger than sitting-type vehicles.

Most ambulance services for day hospitals studied in our survey used more than one type of vehicle. However, when an ambulance driver was asked which particular vehicle he used to transport day hospital patients, his reply would relate to the vehicle used on that particular day.

The vehicles used by the 59 drivers interviewed were reported to be

multipurpose	22 day hospitals
sitting-type	5 day hospitals
minibus	3 day hospitals
cars	1 day hospital

In one day hospital, one driver interviewed was using a multipurpose vehicle on the day of the interview, and the other was using a sitting-type vehicle.

Nine day hospitals had the use of vehicles with a tail-lift. The number of sitting places varied between three (in private cars) and 18 in one large minibus. Most had between six and eight places, some had between nine and 12 places, and only one or two had fewer than six or more than 12 places.

Drivers' views

All the drivers using sitting-type vehicles, minibuses or private cars felt that these were best. Of the 41 drivers using multipurpose vehicles, only 15 thought these were the most suitable. All but two of the 25 drivers who were dissatisfied with multipurpose vehicles elaborated further. Most mentioned poor access to the vehicle; some specified that this was because the vehicle had no tail-lift. Four drivers referred to uncomfortable or unsafe seating as the main disadvantage. Three mentioned that the patients had a poor view from the windows from this vehicle and two drivers thought that the vehicle was too large.

When drivers were asked what would be the alternative to the vehicle they were using, the most frequent answer (17) was 'a vehicle with a tail-lift'; eight drivers specified a sitting-type vehicle or a minibus and five suggested a vehicle with space for wheelchairs. Other suggestions were clear windows and better seating—two drivers thought that angled seats would be better than bench-type seats, and another thought front-facing seats would be best. One driver preferred fewer seats for better access, and one considered that cars were the best vehicles to bring patients to the day hospital.

The drivers who thought that the vehicle they were driving was the one best suited to day hospital patients were asked why this was so. Eleven of these were using multipurpose vehicles. Two said that these were best because they were equipped for emergency, and one found the access to these vehicles and the room they had was better than a sitting-type. Two drivers said it was the most comfortable vehicle for the patients and one commented that the drivers could see them more easily. Two drivers thought it was the most suitable because it had a tail-lift. Three mentioned the adaptability of the multipurpose vehicle and the possibility of carrying patients with any kind of disability.

All ten drivers of sitting-type vehicles gave reasons why they thought them best. Six referred to the tail-lift and the others thought the seating arrangement was more comfortable for the patient. The two drivers using hospital cars were both semi-retired, part-time men, who were not trained ambulance drivers. Cars were the means of transport for patients to this day hospital and were said to be best because of comfort and ease of access. One of the drivers made the point that a car is a more 'personal' means of transport. He thought that patients were more used to cars and that there was less association with illness in a car ride than in an ambulance ride.

Four of the six minibus drivers gave reasons for preferring them. Three thought the seating was the most comfortable and the fourth commented that it was more efficient to use a large vehicle for day hospital runs because it could carry more patients.

One driver commented that there was no one ideal vehicle for every patient. This may well be so, but we felt that the ambulance drivers had given many good suggestions which could be universally adopted.

front-facing or angled permanent seating

room for manoeuvre within the vehicle and perhaps space in which one or two wheelchairs could be secured

access by side entrance with steps for fairly ambulant patients

tail-lift at the rear for the more disabled patients

large clear windows to give patients a good view.

Vehicles probably need to accommodate quite severely disabled, as well as ambulant, patients and might therefore need two drivers. Whilst the most efficient runs would be achieved by large vehicles, we agree with Hildick-Smith that perhaps not more than ten places should be provided in each vehicle or the run would become too prolonged.[38]

Ambulance drivers were asked at what time they usually collected the first patients in the mornings. They replied as follows: before 8.30am for seven day hospitals; 8.30–9.00am for 22 day hospitals; and 9.00–9.30am for three day hospitals. No drivers began to pick up patients after 9.30am.

They were also asked if there were any problems in collecting patients and getting them into the ambulance. Most of them (38 drivers) said there were problems, usually because patients were not ready when the ambulance called.

It's not our job to get patients ready, but there's usually no one else to do it.

We have to help get patients ready—it's part of the job.

Sometimes patients are not ready and we have to go back for them.

Sometimes we have to leave them behind.

About a third of the problems related to difficulty in finding and gaining access to flats, particularly in high-rise blocks, or to difficulties the more disabled patients had in getting into ambulances with no tail-lift. Other problems mentioned were disruption by emergency calls and, in one instance, by occasionally inclement weather.

There were also problems about receiving and passing information between drivers and the day hospital staff. Six drivers complained about being given wrong information by the day hospital about the patients they were to pick up. Four others complained, though non-specifically, about poor communication. One driver said that he never saw the day hospital staff because he left the patients with the hospital porters who then accompanied them to the day hospital which was some distance from the main entrance. Another driver said that he sometimes passed information on to the day hospital staff, which he felt they ignored. Yet we have noted that most of the day hospital staff interviewed thought the ambulancemen were very helpful in passing information to them about problems which patients were having at home.

The men were asked if they liked the work for the day hospital compared with their other work: 26 said they did, but 28 did not and the remainder either did not know or did not answer. Those who gave positive replies were asked what they liked about it, and over half of their replies related to the patients. They liked working with elderly patients as a group and enjoyed 'helping the old folks'. A quarter said the day hospital work was fairly routine and predictable and they liked that. The other replies were rather non-specific; *'It's part of the job'* or *'I like a variety of work including this'.*

Those who did not like day hospital work were asked why. Twenty of them complained that their skills as ambulancemen were not being used. *'I prefer emergency work because it's what I'm trained for'* or *'I'm an ambulanceman, not a bus driver'.* Five drivers simply said they found the work monotonous and boring.

Many of the drivers seemed to find it difficult to answer the questions and our impression was that most of them accepted day hospital work as part of the job but also wanted to be able to do emergency work. There were a few drivers, however, who seemed to prefer day hospital work to any other. One driver commented, *'If a job were advertised for just driving day hospital patients, I would apply for it'.*

Finally, drivers were asked if they were ever directed to do other work when they were scheduled to transport day hospital patients. Fifty drivers answered: 16 said they were not, 20 said they were occasionally and 14 said this happened quite often. These two groups were from 22 of the 30 day hospitals. We did not, however, enquire about how much disruption of day hospital work this actually caused.

From informal conversations with the drivers, we got a variety of opinion about what they believed was the function of the day hospital. Many thought it essentially a social club rather than a treatment centre. If this belief is widespread, it would account for the relatively low priority which ambulance services give to day hospitals compared with other hospital departments. Since the ambulance service is so important to the effectiveness of the day hospital, this would be a useful subject to investigate. The cooperation of ambulance drivers is to be fostered and it seems that the liaison officer, who has been established in some day hospitals, could be very useful. Ambulance drivers are an important link between the day hospital and the patient's home. We would question whether this link is fully appreciated in day hospitals, or indeed fully exploited.

10
Design

Summary

Half of the day hospitals visited were purpose-built and half used adapted premises. Over all, 47 per cent of the staff were satisfied with the structure and layout of the day hospitals: of these, 74 per cent worked in purpose-built day hospitals, but only 17 per cent worked in adapted premises. The complaints of those who were dissatisfied related mainly to poor layout or lack of space. Facilities were said to be adequate by 74 per cent of staff working in purpose-built day hospitals and by 17 per cent of those working in adapted premises.

Various designs for purpose-built units are discussed, including the open-plan arrangement.*

Most of the day hospitals visited were easily classified into two categories: adapted and purpose-built premises. Some hospitals used both, but where a large purpose-built extension provided

*The sketch plans and architects' plans of the day hospitals described in this chapter may be obtained on loan from the library of the King's Fund Centre, 126 Albert Street, London NW1 7NF.

most of the facilities the day hospital was classed as purpose-built; and where most facilities were provided by premises previously in use for some other purpose with an extension providing a minor extra part, the day hospital was classified as adapted. Using this rather empirical approach, we found that half (15) the day hospitals visited were purpose-built and half were adapted. (See also Appendix.)

Staff working in these two kinds of day hospital had very different views on the suitability of the facilities. Over all, 47 per cent of staff were satisfied with the structure and layout of their day hospital. The usual complaint of the remainder was that the day hospital lacked space or that the design was unsatisfactory. The comparison of views was as follows.

	purpose-built %	adapted %
structure satisfactory	74	17
lack of space	19	58
poor design	7	25

Similar replies were received from individual members of staff concerning facilities particularly relevant to their own disciplines; for example, the physicians' consulting and examination facilities; the nurses' treatment rooms, bathrooms and lavatories; the physiotherapists' gymnasium and physical treatment area; and the occupational therapists' workshop and ADL facilities. In purpose-built day hospitals, 74 per cent of staff were satisfied with their facilities. The main dissenters were the physiotherapists; only 53 per cent thought that their facilities were fully adequate. Their major complaint was lack of space to use as an exercise area. In the adapted units, only 17 per cent of staff were fully satisfied, 58 per cent considered that important basic facilities were lacking and 25 per cent were rather more vaguely critical. Most of the staff working in adapted premises, however, were quick to make the point that they gave the patients the best possible treatment within the limitation of the facilities, and that they would far rather have adapted premises, albeit lacking in space, than no day hospital at all.

Virtually any accommodation can serve as a basic day hospital provided that there is one room of reasonable proportions together with lavatories and bathrooms. Perhaps the most basic of day hospitals is the one attached to the Lluesty Hospital, Holywell, North Wales. It is a small converted chapel. At one end of the room is a stage, the space at one side of the stage being used as an office and at the other as a treatment room and lavatory. At the other end is the main entrance with a bathroom and lavatory to one side and a kitchen at the other. These can be used for ADL assessment when necessary. The remainder of the day hospital consists of an open area which is used for physiotherapy and occupational therapy classes as well as a sitting room and dining room. Although this day hospital is able to accommodate only six to eight patients daily, it is very active with a high turnover of patients despite its lack of facilities and a very limited amount of physiotherapy being given. No doubt this is partly attributable to the enthusiasm and efforts of doctors and other members of staff, the sister-in-charge herself taking exercise classes with patients as well as her other duties.

Other adapted day hospitals visited had been converted from hospital chapels, an old schoolroom, an old laundry and the former cellar of an old geriatric hospital. Many of these conversions were quite ingenious in their use of space, and many members of staff cheerfully made do with makeshift facilities. At Pine Heath Day Hospital, Holt, Norfolk, the only possible space for exercises in walking is a corridor connecting the day hospital to the main hospital and this is used to the full. At St Margaret's Day Hospital, Durham, the bathroom is shared with an adjacent ward. Similar compromises were necessary in many of the adapted day hospitals, but lack of space was almost always said to be the major problem. The day hospital at Newsham General Hospital, Liverpool, was started in a large chapel and subsequently expanded by incorporating an adjacent hall, linked by an extension. The consultant and staff all thought that this structure was ideal because it gave plenty of space for patients to move around. There is a separate dining room which also doubles as a gymnasium. Such large buildings, which may adapt well as adequate day hospitals, are perhaps not so often available now on hospital sites, but sites nearby may sometimes be used, as Baker and Clunn describe in their paper, *How they turned a church hall into a day hospital.*[7]

Limited attention has been given in the literature to the design of day hospitals. Cosin, in his paper, *Architectural and functional planning for a geriatric day hospital*[16], described the design of the first purpose-built day hospital in the geriatric service at Oxford which was planned around 1954 and opened in 1958. The emphasis was on catering for the increasing numbers of elderly, confused patients in the community, and the day hospital was therefore planned around a long corridor allowing patients to wander without interference or restriction. The services were central and the treatment rooms circumferential. Physiotherapy treatment rooms were available, but the corridor was used for remedial exercises. The usefulness of the garden with its terrace and lawn was stressed. In the main, other references to the design of day hospitals are included in the large number of papers describing function.* Goldstone, however, has given a very good description of the features which should be included in a day hospital.[30] A summary of her brief may be listed as follows.

1 Entrance with good access for ambulances and cars, with covered area.

*See Chapter 3, Review of literature, pages 9–32.

2 Area with chairs inside entrance where patients can rest on arrival and where wheelchairs and walking aids should be stored.

3 Lavatories and cloakroom near the entrance.

4 One lavatory to five patients—some wide enough for wheelchairs; others, for ambulant patients, should have handrails on the walls. At least one lavatory should have a handrail on the back wall for the occasional patient who transfers forwards onto the lavatory seat from a wheelchair.

5 Bathrooms should have a variety of baths and showers.

6 Treatment room of adequate size.

7 Separate room with lavatory and sluice, for giving an enema.

8 Separate room for physiotherapy exercises; and separate occupational therapy department with good ADL assessment facilities (taking into account the needs of patients in wheelchairs), good area for diversional work with ample storage space and a workshop, and with a launderette and hairdressing room.

9 Proper facilities for the speech therapist and chiropodist.

10 One or more rooms for confidential interviews.

11 Dining room and separate quiet room.

12 Shop—run by volunteers.

13 Staff facilities with locker room, changing room and rest room.

14 Sizeable room for meetings.

The architect should be given precise information on such matters as the height of windows and working surfaces, and a detailed brief for the design of lavatories. An architect, L J Ellis, has stressed the importance of a detailed brief and discussed some of the difficulties of providing what everyone wants within the accommodation available.[24]

One purpose-built day hospital, in Bolton, which all staff working there seemed to like very much, was constructed to the design recommended by the North West Regional Health Authority. This is an entirely self-contained unit separated from the main hospital buildings, and has excellent facilities with treatment rooms, lavatories, accommodation for those members of staff who work only a few sessions at the day hospital such as social workers, speech therapists, hairdressers, chiropodists and opticians, and adequate facilities for all staff.

Complaints about inadequate facilities for staff were common in the purpose-built hospitals and it seems that in many cases insufficient attention had been given to the need for a common room, changing rooms and lavatories. There were some reservations from therapists about having a large open area roughly subdivided into areas for dining and sitting, for occupational therapy (with adjacent ADL assessment area) and for physiotherapy. Therapists working in open-plan accommodation sometimes felt that they would have preferred a separate gymnasium and occupational therapy workshop leading off the general area rather than being an integral part of it.

Burton House Day Hospital, Manchester, has been devised partly out of existing buildings, but the large extension containing a dining room and sitting area, reception area and gymnasium provides clearly defined, separate areas for the physiotherapists and occupational therapists, and several treatment rooms and examination cubicles. One excellent feature is that sister's office has a good view of the dining/sitting area, and the superintendent physiotherapist's office has a view of the gymnasium. Many day hospital staff, especially nurses, complained that their offices were separate from the areas where patients spent their time so that the staff could not observe the patients properly. Another feature at Burton House is the two raised garden areas which are largely paved. At some day hospitals, similar courtyards or gardens were hardly ever used and were regarded as wasted space; at others they were said to be an excellent facility for the summer months.

A particularly impressive design is that of St Thomas' geriatric day hospital, at the South Western Hospital, London. This was designed to serve the dual function of day hospital and day centre, and hence facilities for recreation are incorporated as well as for treatment. These are very spacious and well equipped, particularly the large gymnasium.

Several day hospitals in new geriatric units occupy the ground floor of a ward block, and their design has been dictated to some extent by the design of the ward. The day hospitals at Dudley Road Hospital, Birmingham, and Hinchinbrooke Hospital, Huntingdon, are of this type, and are very similar in basic design, with an open-plan area to one side for sitting and dining, physiotherapy and occupational therapy (where the ward bays would have been), and treatment rooms, examination rooms and lavatories on the other side (where similar services and side wards would have been).

A more complex design is found on the ground floor of the new geriatric block at the Victoria Infirmary, Glasgow. Apart from incorporating a day hospital, the outpatient clinics are held there, and the x-ray department is on the same floor.

At Bexhill, Hastings, a single-storey ward area and day hospital/ rehabilitation unit have been built together on one floor. Here the reception desk is centrally placed between the two parts of the unit, and therefore the receptionist has a very important coordinating role.

There is probably no ideal design for a purpose-built day hospital. So much depends on the ideas of those running the unit and on the site available. We would suggest the following features, however. It is important to have an entrance giving good access to ambulances, with a canopy to protect patients from the weather. The reception area should be large enough to accommodate several patients and have a cloakroom and storage place for wheelchairs and walking aids. Very large reception areas, however, are probably a waste of space. The general purposes/sitting area should offer facilities for diversional work, and there should be a separate quiet room. A separate dining room with its kitchen/servery is generally much better than having a sitting area double as a dining room. There should be separate areas for physiotherapy and occupational therapy with a clear division between the two. Disputes over territory arose between staff using some of the open-plan areas, although usually they were fairly good-natured. The physiotherapy and occupational therapy departments in one hospital were separated by mobile parallel bars, which tended to be moved in one direction or the other depending on which department was feeling short of space at the time. Physiotherapy space was often cramped, as were ADL assessment facilities, while space for diversional work was often unnecessarily generous.

Therapists' and nurses' offices should be planned to give a view of the areas relevant to the occupant, although some staff said that too good a view encouraged too much sitting in offices! The treatment rooms and consulting rooms can be separate from the main areas and should be adequate in number. Many nurses thought that a separate room for giving an enema was needed (with a lavatory leading off) as well as a 'clean' treatment room. Rooms are also required for the speech therapist and occasional visitors, such as hairdresser, chiropodist, optician and dentist, though the functions of such rooms can reasonably be doubled up. At least one room should be set aside for interviews.

There should be a room of adequate size for conferences, meetings and teaching, and adequate lavatories and cloakrooms for staff and patients. Whether the latter should be in two large central units or scattered in various parts of the day hospital is a debatable point. It should not be possible to see into the lavatories from the main entrance to the unit, although there must be room for wheelchairs to get in.

A bathroom is necessary (apart from the assessment bathroom for the occupational therapists), and it may be useful to have both a tub (with room for a hoist) and a 'sitting' bath (Medic-bath). Many nurses thought that showers were of doubtful value, because old people are generally much happier with a soak in a tub. If a shower is provided, it must enable patients to shower sitting down, in such a position that they avoid getting their hair wet.

Many purpose-built units had a laundry room with an automatic washing machine. This was usually regarded as useful for incontinent patients, for whom a small clothing store was also very important, but the original idea that patients would do their own washing has hardly ever worked. Very few elderly people seemed to be prepared to learn how to use an automatic machine.

There was some criticism in day hospitals oriented to rehabilitation about providing facilities with a 'day centre flavour' such as a television in the lounge or a hairdressing room. In the main, however, such facilities were regarded as being useful, if not essential, parts of the day hospital.

The importance of the correct height of windows, the adequate width of some lavatories for wheelchairs, may seem self-evident, but must be discussed carefully by the team members working on a day hospital design, or the complaint, 'Why can't day hospitals be designed by the people working in them?' will be heard again and again.

11

Costs

Summary

The running costs of 23 day hospitals in 1977 are analysed: 12 have been costed by questionnaire based on functional accounts; three finance departments presented both a subjective and a functional analysis for their day hospitals.

In day hospitals presenting subjective accounts, the mean expenditure on staffing was £7.67 per patient attendance (range £4.07 to £12.93). The mean non-staff expenditure was £2.32 per patient attendance (range £1.01 to £3.54). Mean total expenditure was £9.99 per patient attendance (excluding ambulance costs).

In those day hospitals presenting functional accounts only, the mean total expenditure was £10.37 per patient attendance (excluding ambulance costs). The mean cost per new patient was £389.59.

In 15 day hospitals, the mean cost of ambulance transport was £3.20 per patient attendance (range £2.07 to £4.79).

The day patient attendance costs, on average, 60 per cent of the inpatient day (range 49–81 per cent), excluding ambulance costs. Adding ambulance costs, the day patient attendance costs, on average, 78 per cent of the inpatient day.

The cost of a course of treatment at the day hospital (that is, the cost per new day patient) was, on average, 70 per cent of the cost of an inpatient course of treatment, excluding transport. With transport cost included, the cost of a course of day hospital treatment was, on average, 89 per cent of the cost for an in-patient stay.

As the methods of accounting vary, however, no precise conclusions can be drawn from the figures obtained. The problems of obtaining comparable accounts between day hospitals, and between day patients and inpatients, are discussed.

The point is made that, for day patients, secondary costs (of community services) and tertiary costs (of running a home) would require to be considered in formulating a complete costing of treatment as a day patient. Thus, it is suggested that comparison of day patient and inpatient treatment is not really valid.

In the National Health Service, patients and practitioners are not cost-conscious since there is at present no way by which the realities of costing can be brought home to them. Perhaps the only exception is the practice, over a number of years, by which the Department of Health and Social Security has sent leaflets to all the doctors in the NHS showing comparative prices of pharmaceutical preparations.

The realistic costing of a day hospital as a separate element within the geriatric service is incredibly complex. The detailed discussion of cost analysis in geriatric day care by Doherty and Hicks has been referred to in Chapter 2.[20] Analysis of costs in the day hospitals studied in the manner suggested by these authors is beyond the scope of the present survey, which is confined to a determination of the primary or direct cost of day care in some of the hospitals visited.

Standard accounting practice in the NHS since its reorganisation in 1974 has been to produce 'functional' accounts based on the cost of services rather than of staff and materials. Such accounts detail the expenditure on direct services to patients, and medical and paramedical supporting services (including diagnostic services such as radiology and electrocardiography, and treatment such as physiotherapy, occupational therapy, chiropody), and general services (administration, domestic, catering, laundry). Before 1974, NHS accounts were usually presented under so-called 'subjective' headings which included the salaries of various groups of staff, with materials and equipment shown under separate headings.

After discussion with staff working in the finance office of a large health district, we decided that a more accurate breakdown of the running costs of day hospitals would be obtained by requesting details of costs under a series of such 'subjective' headings. Information was also requested on the number of new patients seen in the day hospital over the year and on the total number of attendances over the year, in order to determine a cost per patient per attendance. Where appropriate, we also asked for details of costs for inpatients for comparison.

A number of difficulties soon became apparent. Some finance officers could not supply accounts for the day hospital in their health district because it was too small for separate costing (less than 5000 attendances annually), and the running costs were shown as part of the costs for the outpatient departments. Further, in some of these small hospitals, the precise commitment of staff working with both inpatients and day patients was not specified, and could not therefore be costed. Indeed, in many larger units which served as rehabilitation areas for inpatients and outpatients, there was some difficulty in apportioning the commitment to day patients. For example, in Burton House Day Hospital, sessions by medical staff relate solely to day patients, whereas sessions by nursing staff relate both to day patients and to inpatients attending for rehabilitation. Enquiries suggested that some 75 per cent of nursing time was in fact spent with day patients in nursing procedures and general care. But for inpatients, nursing procedures were carried out in the wards and only general care was undertaken in the day hospital. On the other hand, the remedial therapists estimated that they spent only 40 per cent of their time with day patients and 60 per cent with inpatients. Clerical staff at the day hospital were engaged in work concerning day patients for virtually the whole of their time.

The same problems were apparent when costing 'non-staff' expenditure. Whereas catering services in the day hospital were divided between day patients and inpatients on the basis of the mean ratio of the two, the cost of drugs and dressings related solely to day patients. The cost of transport by ambulance also given as 'non-staff' expenditure relates solely to the day patients.

The annual running costs of Burton House Day Hospital are shown in Table 19. Other finance officers pointed out ambiguities in the 'subjective' questionnaire, especially with regard to transport. Our intention was to establish the cost of ambulance transport under this heading, but this is costed at regional level, and district finance officers usually gave the cost of transport within the hospital, namely portering and internal ambulance services. Some ascertained an approximate cost of the ambulance service for the day hospital on the basis of figures supplied by the regional health authority; in other instances we obtained this information by a separate approach to the regional authority. In some areas, information was offered about the costs of day hospitals other than the one being investigated, and some of this information has been included in our analysis in order to give as representative a picture as possible. Clearly the task of determining accurate running costs for a day hospital is a complex one, and we

Table 19 Annual running costs of Burton House Day Hospital (45 places)

	whole-time equivalents	*expenditure* £	*percentage apportioned to day patients*	*expenditure on day patients* £
Staff				
medical	1	6 188	100	6 188
nursing	8.75	29 682	75	22 261.50
professional/technical	17.35	58 439	40	23 375.60
administrative/clerical	3	8 804	100	8 804
building/engineering	–	–	–	–
other	4.27	10 071	40	4 028.40
Non-staff				
catering		6 193	40	2 477.20
staff uniforms		832	40	332.80
patients' clothing		200	100	200
drugs		5 837	100	5 837
dressings/appliances/equipment		6 124	50	3 062
general services		3 865	40	1 546
maintenance, engineering, grounds		4 157	40	1 662.80
domestic repairs, renewals		1 410	40	564
other a rates		1 735	40	694
b transport		25 769	100	25 769
c all other		200	40	80
		£169 506		£106 882.30

must pay tribute to those finance officers and members of their staff who carried out a very complex analysis of costs in response to our request, particularly those in smaller units.

In the day hospitals where expenditure was detailed under 'subjective' headings, staff expenditure was obviously the major item. In some cases there was an over-estimate of the actual cost, because staff had not been recruited up to the permitted establishment, or because the commitment of staff to day patients had been over-estimated. For example, in one day hospital, the physiotherapy establishment was equal to 2.75 whole-time physiotherapists and costs were given accordingly. In fact there were only two physiotherapy sessions weekly in that day hospital, which were undertaken by a part-time remedial gymnast. In others, there was an under-estimate. For example, in one day hospital, no expenditure was shown for medical staff because it was the practice for the consultant to make sporadic short visits with no other doctor being involved. However, a recently appointed senior registrar was in fact spending a full session weekly in the day hospital, unknown to the finance officer.

Cost analysis from subjective questionnaire

Completed subjective questionnaires were received for 15 day hospitals. These are probably fairly representative of day hospitals as a whole, the annual attendance figures varying from 424 at the smallest to 12477 at the largest, with a mean annual attendance of 7061. There is obviously a tremendous variation in the total annual expenditure at these hospitals on both staff and non-staff expenditure, and it is not therefore useful to compare total expenditure of one hospital with another. The figures given in Table 20 simply illustrate the very considerable expenditure on day hospitals, particularly on staffing. With a mean total annual cost of staff at day hospitals of £48070 (ranging from £5483 to £95961), and a mean total expenditure of £66994 (with a range

Table 20 Cost analysis of 15 day hospitals (by subjective questionnaire)

	Annual expenditure			*Cost per patient attendance*		
	Range		*Mean*	*Range*		*Mean*
	£	£	£	£	£	£
Staff						
medical	–	11 096	4 451	–	1.16	0.55
nursing	1 991	36 807	19 405	1.64	4.70	2.88
professional and technical	1 206	23 376	11 350	0.33	5.40	2.38
administrative and clerical	195	9 000	3 827	0.12	1.25	0.52
building and engineering	–	8 879	1 702	–	1.20	0.22
other	–	18 187	7 335	–	2.20	1.12
total (staff)	£5 483	£95 961	£48 070	£4.07	£12.93	£7.16
Non-staff						
catering	270	8 926	3 552	0.28	1.04	0.53
staff uniforms	–	500	155	–	0.06	0.02
patients' clothing	–	200	48	–	0.03	0.01
drugs	–	6 665	1 939	–	0.90	0.23
dressings	–	923	627	–	0.08	0.02
medical/surgical appliances and equipment	–	6 894	1 229	–	0.60	0.15
general services	–	11 600	3 543	–	0.98	0.40
maintenance of grounds and buildings	69	12 136	4 430	0.02	1.64	0.50

continued on next page

domestic repairs, renewals	–	1 900	441	–	0.16	0.05
rates	29	7 152	1 627	0.05	0.83	0.18
internal transport	–	2 100	284	–	0.18	0.04
other	–	3 258	1 049	–	1.01	0.19
total (non-staff)	£1 078	£33 600	£18 924	£1.01	£3.54	£2.32
Grand total	£6 562	£119 959	£66 994	£6.04	£15.48	£9.99

between £6562 and £119 959), it can readily be seen that day hospitals are consuming a significant proportion of the resources of the NHS.

In comparing expenditure between hospitals by the cost per patient's attendance, one might expect this to be fairly uniform, but in fact, as the table shows, there is great variation. The mean cost of medical staffing in the day hospital was 55p for each patient's attendance. Expenditure on nursing staff was the biggest single item (apart from ambulance transport, which will be discussed later). The next most expensive group was the professional and technical staff, mostly physiotherapists and occupational therapists. It is worth noting that there was some tendency for expenditure on professional and technical staff to be inversely proportional to expenditure on nursing staff. Martin and Millard have argued, from their study on three day hospitals[53], that where nursing staff predominate the hospital is likely to have an essentially custodial function, whereas when remedial staff predominate the function is likely to be more rehabilitative. They consider, therefore, that a higher ratio of remedial staff to nursing staff would be desirable in most day hospitals.

There was considerable variation, too, in expenditure on the three other groups of staff. All the returns received costed some of the time spent by administrative and clerical staff. Presumably in those hospitals where such expenditure was small, a good deal of the administrative work would be carried out by the nursing staff. Four hospitals gave no expenditure on building and engineering staff, and two hospitals gave no expenditure on 'other' staff, who would include domestic staff and porters. The latter expenditure was costed in general services and internal transport.

Non-staff expenditure also showed great variation. That for catering services is partly due to the inclusion of catering staff costs in some returns and not in others. The mean of 53p per patient per attendance would have been pushed up significantly by a return from one day hospital which gave a total cost for catering in the day hospital of £31 038. At this hospital the cost of catering per patient per attendance comes to almost £3, very much more than at any of the others. Other returns from this hospital were somewhat suspect and, as no satisfactory explanation was obtained, these returns have been excluded from the analysis.

Three hospitals gave no returns for staff uniforms and one hospital costed these and patients' clothing together. All hospitals gave a cost for at least one of the items, drugs, dressings, and medical and surgical appliances and equipment, but one returned no expenditure on drugs, two returned none on dressings and one returned none on medical and surgical appliances and equipment. At one hospital a combined cost for all three headings was given; in another the cost of dressing and appliances and equipment was combined; and in a third the cost of drugs and dressings was combined. All this makes it difficult to interpret the returns, but it certainly seems that there is great variation. For example, the cost of drugs, where a figure has been detailed, varied from 1p to 90p per patient per attendance, and appliances and equipment from 1p to 60p. All hospitals gave a return for maintenance of buildings and grounds but again there was great variation. Four hospitals gave no expenditure for domestic repairs, renewals and replacements, whilst three spent more than £1000 a year. This expenditure may have been due more to dilapidation than to the size of the unit, since the cost tended to be higher in the adapted premises than in the purpose-built hospitals.

Variation in local rates requires no explanation, the rates paid for one rural day hospital amounting only to £29.23 a year, whereas for a day hospital in a large city the rates were £7152 a year. The cost of internal transport varies considerably because costs of porters have sometimes been included. (The cost of ambulance transport to the day hospital is discussed below.) Three units gave no 'other' expenditure, and all were less than 50p per patient per attendance with one exception at £1.01–this hospital had not given full costs under other headings. The table shows that non-staff expenditure is only one-third of the cost of staff, and no doubt if all the staffing component were taken out of the returns under non-staff expenditure, which some day hospitals gave, the proportion would be even smaller. The grand total expenditure ranges from £6.04 for one of the larger hospitals with 6966 attendances a year to £15.48 for the smallest with 424 attendances a year. Martin and Millard have stated that the smaller the unit the more efficient it tends to become.[53] We cannot, of course, comment on the cost-effectiveness of the hospitals for which we have returns, but certainly in terms of cost-efficiency the small day hospital comes out badly.

Cost analysis on functional accounting

The functional accounts for 11 day hospitals are analysed in Table 21. Three of these were units which had also presented an analysis of costs on the basis of the 'subjective' questionnaire, and we comment below on the comparison between the two systems in these three units. Functional accounts were also received for day patients at three other hospitals but have not been included in our analysis, since at these hospitals the costs for all day patients were presented together, whether they were attending the geriatric day hospital, the psychiatric day hospital or another unit. For example, one return included renal patients attending every day, and obviously such returns would not be comparable with those dealing solely with patients attending a geriatric day hospital.

Again, there was considerable variation in both size and function and we feel that they are probably fairly representative of day hospitals as a whole. They had a mean annual attendance of 8494 (ranging from 3112 to 14 108). In most instances the functional accounts give not only the cost of a service per patient per attendance but a cost for each case, which is derived by dividing the total expenditure by the number of new patients attending the day hospital over the year. One could criticise the derivation of a cost per patient in the day hospital in this way, but the figures derived may go some little way towards indicating cost-effectiveness rather than cost-efficiency.

Salaries of medical staff appeared as an item of expenditure in all but one of the 11 day hospitals, the mean expenditure being £21.45 per case or 59p per patient per attendance. Variation again was quite considerable, the highest cost being £1.12 per attendance. This was not, however, the hospital with the highest cost per patient for medical staffing, and it might well be valid to argue that a high cost for medical staffing for each attendance is offset by the higher turnover of patients which this induces.

Nursing services were again the single most expensive item. It is perhaps worth noting that there was no relationship between the expenditure on nursing services and the number of new patients seen annually at the day hospital.

All 11 day hospitals gave figures for the cost of supplies and equipment, but in one hospital the cost per patient per attendance was so small that we disregarded it.

Table 21 Cost analysis of 11 day hospitals (by functional accounting)

	Total expenditure			*Cost per new day patient*			*Cost per attendance*		
	Range		*Mean*	*Range*		*Mean*	*Range*		*Mean*
	£	£	£	£	£	£	£	£	£
Patient care services									
medical	–	11 248	4 502	–	57.69	21.45	–	1.12	0.59
nursing	300	57 967	19 742	3.19	203.39	106.48	0.05	4.84	3.18
supplies and equipment	15	18 159	3 972	0.16	61.35	35.35	–	1.29	0.46
total	£1 315	£71 420	£28 216	£8.26	£250.59	£163.28	£0.17	£5.97	£4.23
Medical and paramedical support services									
diagnostic	–	2 445	749	–	8.26	1.99	–	0.42	0.10
physiotherapy	–	14 886	2 327	–	43.53	13.43	–	2.50	0.42

occupational therapy	–	19 563	7 178	–	49.21	23.31	–	2.47	0.97
other	–	1 516	387	–	16.53	2.86	–	0.29	0.07
total	£235	£29 887	£10 641	£1.41	£87.39	£41.59	£0.03	£5.02	£1.56
General services									
administration, records and training	218	11 908	5 288	2.32	62.96	23.86	0.04	1.68	0.73
catering	1 089	19 454	5 968	15.65	68.26	30.81	0.35	1.15	0.78
cleaning, portering, laundry	1 683	35 470	13 578	28.02	203.18	71.33	0.54	4.57	1.66
estate management	897	33 025	10 807	15.20	198.94	55.76	0.25	4.47	1.31
other	–	2 417	788	–	8.48	2.96	–	0.28	0.10
total	£1 064	£95 400	£36 429	£70.53	£482.07	£184.72	£1.86	£10.83	£4.58
Grand total	£17 295	£183 202	£75 286	£183.99	£661.58	£389.49	£2.82	£15.32	£10.37

The most striking variations were the costs of medical and para-medical supporting services. Four of the 11 hospitals showed no expenditure on diagnostic services (radiology, pathology, electro-cardiography) when in fact in at least three of these there is no doubt that day patients were using diagnostic services.

Physiotherapy and occupational therapy are also costed under the heading of supporting services and, again, showed a great deal of variation. As with nursing costs, there was no relationship between expenditure on remedial therapy services and the number of new patients seen in the day hospital. However, we seriously doubt the accuracy of the expenditure returns in some cases. Three day hospitals showed no expenditure on physiotherapy, yet in two of them we saw physiotherapists treating patients at the time of our visits. Only one hospital showed no expenditure on occupational therapy, but this was one of those which had shown no expenditure on physiotherapy or on diagnostic services. Since it was a large and extremely active day hospital, it was indeed surprising that the finance department did not seem to be aware of its activities. The same hospital gave no expenditure on catering for patients. A small expenditure was shown for catering for staff. It would seem that the finance department did not know that patients were getting a midday meal in the day hospital. In any event, it is a serious distortion of the expenditure on this day hospital. The cost of these services provided in the day hospital appeared, at least in part, in the cost returns for the hospital inpatients, pushing up the apparent costs per day for inpatients and cutting down considerably the cost per day patient per attendance. Had this day hospital been costed properly it is possible that the cost per day for inpatients and for day patients per attendance would have been comparable. In fact, the accounts show the cost per day patient per attendance as 56 per cent of the cost per day per inpatient.

'Other' expenditure on supporting services such as speech therapy, social work and chiropody, again varied considerably and again was often inaccurately costed. We know that two hospitals had established speech therapy sessions, but these showed no expenditure on speech therapy. The mean total expenditure on medical and paramedical supporting services was considerably less than on general care of patients (£1.56 per patient per attendance compared with £4.23 per patient per attendance).

Expenditure on general services requires little comment. As already noted, one finance department omitted to cost catering for patients in the day hospital, but otherwise an item of expenditure was recorded for each unit under each heading, with the exception of two hospitals for which no expenditure was recorded. It is of interest to note the variation in expenditure on administration, medical records and training (which are shown together in Table 21) from 4p to £1.68 per patient per attendance, and on estate management, from 25p to £4.47 per patient per attendance. The mean cost of general services per patient per attendance is greater at £4.58 than that of either nursing (£3.18) or medical and paramedical supporting services (£1.56).

The grand total expenditure varied from £2.82 to £15.32, with a mean of £10.37. The day hospital showing the lowest cost per patient per attendance was exceptional; the next lowest cost was £5.56. Of the three hospitals which gave subjective and functional accounts, one showed exact agreement between the two in terms of the total cost per patient per attendance, the other two did not. In one, the cost per attendance given on the functional account was higher, apparently because some staffing costs of general services had been omitted from the replies to the subjective questionnaire. In the other, the subjective questionnaire gave a higher cost per patient per attendance because expenditure was shown for physiotherapy sessions which did not figure in the functional accounts.

Ambulance costs

The cost of transporting patients by ambulance to and from the day hospital was determined in 15 of the hospitals visited. In five of these figures were given for mileage covered in respect of day hospital patients and for cost per mile, and a total expenditure was derived from these two figures. In the other ten, the cost was derived from a figure giving the mean cost per journey for each non-emergency patient carried and the total attendances at the day hospital over the year. The mean cost of transport per patient per attendance was £3.20 (range £2.07 to £4.79). This is a considerable addition to the cost per attendance at the day hospital given by the district finance department and takes the mean total cost per attendance from £9.79 to £12.99 on the subjective analysis, and from £9.57 to £12.77 on the functional analysis.

Comparison with inpatient costs

It is often suggested that day hospitals may be a satisfactory alternative to inpatient hospitals. It is therefore relevant to try to compare the cost of the two kinds of treatment. But we are not comparing like groups of patients, and this casts doubt on any conclusions drawn. Further, it is difficult to determine in precisely what manner the costs for day patients and for inpatients may be compared.

Functional accounts showing the expenditure on inpatients were received for 16 geriatric departments whose day hospitals we visited. In only 10 of these, however, did we consider it appropriate to compare day patient and inpatient costs, because the day hospital was part of a hospital serving mainly elderly patients of whom a significant number were classed as rehabilitation rather than long-stay. In the other six, day patients and inpatients were not comparable groups, usually because the day hospital was part of a district general hospital and the mean costs of inpatients related to all patients—medical, surgical, geriatric, children, or whatever.

Of the 10 sets of accounts, we discovered that the day patient, on average, costs 60 per cent of the inpatient costs, the range being from 49 to 81 per cent. If, however, we add transport costs to the day patient's cost per attendance—either the mean given for the area where this was known or, in the other cases, the mean which we have determined—the day patient per attendance costs 78 per cent of the inpatient per day. This comparison can certainly be criticised on the grounds that the day patient's day and the inpatient's day are not comparable. The average inpatient's day takes account of weekends, and it could be argued that the cost of five days at the day hospital should be compared with the cost of five weekdays for an inpatient.

It might, therefore, be more relevant to compare the cost of a course of treatment for a day patient with a course of treatment for an inpatient. In the 10 day hospitals, the mean number of attendances for a day patient was 45 days (range 20 to 65 days), lower than the mean length of stay per inpatient, which was 68 days (range 19 to 177 days).

Comparing the cost given per patient in the day hospital with the total cost given per inpatient at the same hospital, a course of treatment at the day hospital appeared to cost 70 per cent, on average, of a course of treatment as an inpatient. If a factor is added for transport, the cost per course of day hospital treatment rises to 89 per cent of the inpatient cost. Indeed, treatment as a day patient may be more expensive than treatment as an inpatient if we add to the hospital's cost the costs of home nursing service, home help service, meals on wheels, and other community services which the day patients may be receiving concurrently with their hospital treatment. If to these costs are added those of living at home, the cost of treatment as a day patient probably substantially exceeds the cost of treatment as an inpatient.

However, there is little doubt that treatment as a day patient is very different from treatment as an inpatient. It may relate more closely to independent functioning in the community. It may also be that many day patients much prefer their treatment to the alternative of being admitted to hospital. In retrospect, a useful question to have asked of patients in this survey would have been, 'Would you have preferred to have your course of treatment as an inpatient rather than as a day patient?'.

We believe that it would be fair to say that finance officers whose responsibility it is to undertake the collection of costing information do not always know what goes on in their day hospitals. However, despite the extraordinary range of costs in different day hospitals, it is rather striking that the mean cost calculated by two different methods is almost exactly the same, and, further, is comparable to that calculated by McFarlane and others in their costing study.*

Until there are more uniform methods of collecting information on the effectiveness of day hospital treatment, the questions raised here will remain unanswerable. Only a controlled trial with random allocation of patients to day care or inpatient treatment (along the lines of that designed by Woodford-Williams and others in 1962[81], but on a bigger scale and with more detailed attention to cost comparison, preferably on a multicentre basis) will start to provide the answers.

*See footnote, page 31.

12

Social day centres

Summary

Information about provision of day care was obtained from 23 of the social services departments responsible for the catchment areas of the 30 day hospitals visited. These 23 departments had 50 purpose-built day centres, 52 adapted day centres and 102 residential homes which also offered some day care, but there was a wide variation in facilities. Some transport for day care clients was available in 21 areas, but only for 57 per cent of the day care establishments.

There was a waiting list for day care in 15 areas—the mean waiting time being 6.3 weeks. Meals, handicrafts and games were available in 87 per cent of the day care establishments in the areas investigated. Some kind of assessment of clients was carried out in day care establishments in 15 areas.

Volunteers were deployed in 14 areas.

More than half the social service staff saw day centres as having a function complementary to the day hospital. Many felt that there should be better liaison between the two services.

Although our three surveys were concerned with geriatric day hospitals, it seemed important to pay some attention to day centres, inasmuch as they relate to the work of the day hospital. In the first survey, 85 per cent of geriatricians said they had difficulty in transferring patients to day centres. Yet once day care has started in a day hospital, enjoyment of the companionship—so often in great contrast to the isolation of the rest of the patient's life—quickly becomes established. Indeed, the patient may become dependent upon the day hospital because of this. But this dependency is positive rather than negative: it is the appreciation of a widening of an otherwise rapidly contracting horizon and as such promotes health. What, then, will happen when rehabilitation is complete and there seems no indication to continue maintenance treatment? For many patients, especially those who live alone (37 per cent in our survey), the end of treatment and discharge from the day hospital become something to be feared—or at least regretted. There can be little doubt that many of the patients continuing at day hospitals for social reasons feel this, yet probably many of them could obtain equal benefit (probably more) from a social day centre. The availability of social day centres—the complement of the day hospital—is therefore of importance to those who provide day hospital care. Consequently we tried to discover the availability of statutory social day centres for patients attending the 30 day hospitals studied in our third survey. There is a wealth of voluntary funded and operated types of day care. Many of these, however, are day clubs, luncheon clubs and drop-in clubs which do not provide transport. Where a patient becomes sufficiently mobile to make his own way to a voluntary day centre of any kind, this will almost certainly meet his needs, but if he requires transport in most cases only a statutory day centre will be able to provide it. The day centres we studied were those open for a significant part of the working day.

We found it difficult sometimes to discover which day centres were provided in the catchment area of the various day hospitals and therefore available to their patients. Social service areas do not always match the day hospital catchment area: thus, a day centre might be shared by two different day hospitals, or a day hospital might have more than one day centre in its catchment area. For example, some day hospitals in London share overlapping catchment areas. St Matthew's Day Hospital and Whittington Day Hospital share the facilities of Hackney Borough. St Matthew's also shares with St Pancras Day Hospital the facilities of the Borough of Islington. Two of these day hospitals, St Matthew's and Whittington, have catchment areas which cover parts of three London boroughs. St Matthew's patients can come from Tower Hamlets, Hackney and Islington, and Whittington's patients from Hackney, Haringey and Barnet.

Information was sought by postal questionnaire of the senior social worker in the area concerned through the director of social services. Often this was followed up by telephone or by a visit. We obtained information on the catchment areas of 23 of the 30 day hospitals; some of these replies were incomplete.

The range of day care—both in residential homes and in day centres—in relation to the 23 day hospitals is shown in Table 22. Altogether, there were 50 purpose-built day centres, 52 adapted day centres and 102 residential homes providing day care. The range varied from two day centres with no day care in residential homes in two areas (Glasgow and Guisborough), to 14 day centres with seven residential homes with day care in one area (Nottingham). Six day hospitals each had more than 15 day care establishments in their areas.

Information was supplied on the type of people for whom day care was intended in 118 day care establishments.*

*The term 'day care establishment' covers both day centres and day care in residential homes.

		%
specifically for people of retirement age	46	39
disabled people only of retirement age	3	2.5
mentally confused only of retirement age	9	7.5
elderly people and others	47	40
disabled people of all ages	13	11

Transport

Transport was available in all but two of the 23 areas. Transport was not available for all the establishments in the other areas but some form of transport was provided for 100 of the 196 establishments about which this information was obtained. For 47 of these, the vehicles were social service ambulances, for three they were taxis or private cars and for 50 they were a combination of both types of transport.

Waiting lists

Information about waiting lists for day care establishments was collected from 21 of the 30 day hospitals' catchment areas: 15 had waiting lists, and the time varied from 2 to 15 weeks, the average being 6.3 weeks. The main reasons given were lack of transport and/or lack of day centre places. Another reason was the distance of the patient's home from the establishment which had a vacancy.

Facilities

Meals were available in 87 per cent of the establishments in the 23 areas. Handicrafts and games were also each provided in 87

Table 22 Day care provided by social services departments in 23 day hospital catchment areas

	elderly people's homes providing day care	*day centres available to the day hospital*	*transport*	*waiting list for places*
in London				
St Matthew's	1	6	yes	yes
St Michael's	0	4	yes	yes
St Pancras	3	6	yes	yes
Whittington	2	14	yes	yes
in other cities				
Bolton General	9	9	yes	yes
Burton House, Manchester	0	5	yes	yes
Dudley Road, Birmingham	11	2	yes	yes
Ladywell, Salford	10	7	yes	yes
Newsham, Liverpool	12	4	yes	no
Peterborough	5	3	yes	no
St David's, Cardiff	0	11	yes	yes
St James's, Leeds	–	8	yes	–
Sherwood, Nottingham	7	14	yes	yes
Victoria, Glasgow	0	2	yes	yes
Warrington	6	2	yes	yes
in small towns				
Airedale, Keighley	6	2	no	–
Bexhill	2	1	yes	no
Guisborough	0	2	yes	yes
Maesgwyn, Bridgend	6	2	yes	no
St Margaret's, Durham	5	1	yes	yes
West Park, Macclesfield	10	6	yes	yes
in rural areas				
Hinchinbrooke, Huntingdon	4	9	yes	no
Lluesty, Holywell	3	1	no	no

per cent. Hairdressing was available in 16 areas and a library in 15. Chiropody and occupational therapy were available in all areas. Laundry facilities were provided in five. Establishments in two areas, both industrial cities, offered physiotherapy and speech therapy. Nursing care was available in three areas, although nurses were actually employed as nurses in only one.

Other facilities included adult education programmes, eurhythmics, dancing, films, drama, music, yoga, religious services, outings and opportunities to do light work. In one area welfare counselling was available, in another bathing, and in a third the old people could order groceries and have them delivered to the day centres.

Assessment

In 15 areas assessment was carried out in the day centres. In 11 of these, assessment was physical, mental and social, and in two it was mental and social only. Replies from the other two areas did not specify.

The manager, often with assistance of other staff of the centre or the area social worker, generally made the assessment. In two areas the social services' residential care officer was responsible for assessment, and in three others either a physician, occupational therapist or teacher from a specialised centre for mentally handicapped.

Volunteers

Volunteers helped in day care establishments in 14 areas, most commonly two or three in each day centre. The average number of volunteers working in centres in each area was 14.

Day centres and day hospitals

The social workers were asked about their concept of the role of the day centre in relation to the geriatric day hospital. Twenty-one replied. Eleven stated that the day centre directly complemented the day hospital by providing general support for the elderly, and eight also felt that the day centre was a service which should follow day hospital attendance.

> *An after-care service to clients discharged from day hospital in an effort to maintain them in their own homes.*

> *The day centres ought to be in a position to continue any programme of rehabilitation, social training, etc, started by the day hospital.*

Replies from half the social services departments went into more detail. By providing the elderly with care and support it was hoped that the day centre would contribute to maintaining them in the community for as long as possible. The day centre was seen as being primarily socially oriented, providing old people with opportunities to meet and talk with other people and to be involved in various activities.

> *The day centre is part of a pattern of support services of the social services department providing facilities for care, companionship and social, recreational and occupational activities.*

Three senior social workers described day centres as having primarily the same function as the day hospital. One stated that the role of day care provided by the social services is similar to the day hospital though less health oriented. The other two stressed the need for better links with the hospital service in the care of the elderly, and one of them suggested that there be joint funding and staffing of services for the elderly.

Another suggested that more liaison could take place between the county council and area health authority to provide hospital day care facilities over the weekend to elderly people when day centres are closed. In that area the day hospital already made some provision for a limited amount of day care over the weekend.

It appears from this survey that some day care is available either in day centres or in residential homes in most catchment areas but patients discharged from day hospitals can only use day centres if transport is available. In fact, only 57 per cent of the day care establishments had transport although almost all the day hospital areas had one or more day care establishments providing transport in their areas. The presence of a waiting list in 70 per cent of day centres, compared with 17 per cent of day hospitals, also limits their usefulness. Patients ready for discharge have to continue attending day hospitals after they have reached the stage of discharge. These two factors—transport difficulties and waiting lists—are probably interrelated and between them explain why 85 per cent of geriatricians reported difficulty in transferring patients to day centres.

Though facilities for social day care following patients' discharge from the day hospital are generally available, in most cases either geriatricians must allow their patients to continue attending for some extra weeks until a place turns up or the patient must spend these weeks in a kind of limbo at home—discharged from one type of day care and awaiting the other. What happens no doubt depends on the rigidity with which the geriatrician regards rapid turnover as an essential tenet of his day hospital policy. If waiting time is no more than six weeks this will add only 11 extra attendances per patient over all, having in mind that only 17 per cent of patients discharged require day centre care.

Although data were not obtained on the degree of frailty accepted by social workers as compatible with social day care, it was clear from discussions with social workers, and their general comments, that in a number of areas there is a distinct gap between their view and that of geriatricians. Thus, many patients discharged from day hospitals might not be acceptable clients in the day centre. This certainly applies to incontinent patients, and even to old people who need help to go to the lavatory. Appropriate staff may not be available to help them.

Close liaison and discussion between geriatricians and social workers are essential if a total policy of day care is to be developed. Flexibility is obviously necessary, and if the norms set out by the Department of Health and Social Security for day hospital provision are met[31], there should be adequate scope for it.

Closely related to flexibility is the extent to which social day care centres offer facilities for assessment. There is considerable scope for experiment (and a good example of such experiment is that in the London Borough of Newham[23]) and it is equally important to avoid reduplication of expensive professional services and to be sure that assessment is carried out by appropriately qualified people. It seems unlikely that medical, functional and psychological assessment can be adequate unless physicians and remedial therapists are available (some might add psychologists as well). Again, this would seem to be a matter for local discussion.

The day hospitals associated with St Thomas' and St Matthew's hospitals in London and the Lamellion Day Hospital in Cornwall are important examples of experiments in this area. This whole question of social day care and its relationship to the day hospital is also of particular interest and relevant to developing practice in North America, where it is the subject of some deliberately planned prospective studies.

13
Conclusions and commentary

Purpose of the geriatric day hospital

The first requirement is to establish the purpose of the geriatric day hospital. Planners need to be informed of this in relation to the deployment of resources and the design of buildings. Equally important, people who work in the day hospital need to understand their objectives and to appreciate how their work with individual patients moves towards achieving these objectives. The purpose of a geriatric day hospital is not simple and clear-cut, as is, for instance, the purpose of a family planning clinic. It has a number of quite different objectives; these may apply to different patients at any one time and to any one patient at different times. The staff need to understand the objectives in relation to each patient and to appreciate that the objectives will change for each patient. The reason why any patient is attending the day hospital should be clearly defined by the person who refers the patient, should be reconsidered when the patient first attends and treatment is prescribed, and should be further reconsidered from time to time throughout the patient's period of attendance as his condition (improvement or deterioration) changes.

The reason for attendance and the changing reasons should be clearly stated in the patient's case records, with perhaps supporting evidence on why that is the reason at that time. We found in our visits to day hospitals and in conversation with members of staff at all levels that this is not often done. In many cases the professional staff did not know why patients were attending and there was no indication of the reason in the notes.

The objectives will be viewed differently by professional staff, according to their own contribution. We found that the physicians and physiotherapists were more likely to see active treatment as the main purpose than were nurses and occupational therapists. We also found that the structure of the day hospital affected the staff's perception of its purpose. While 41 per cent of all professional staff regarded active treatment as the main purpose of the day hospital, this varied from 27 per cent of those working in adapted buildings to 54 per cent of those working in purpose-built day hospitals. Most of those working in purpose-built hospitals (81 per cent) felt they were achieving their objectives, whereas this applied to only 66 per cent of those working in adapted day hospitals.

Rehabilitation

Many geriatricians would regard this as their most important objective. It topped the list when geriatricians were asked to place in rank order the various day hospital functions. We have described it in the first chapter as a dynamic and finite process, implying that it should be possible to define the point at which rehabilitation is no longer applicable, the patient having achieved maximum independence.

Assessment

While it is not difficult to understand what assessment means in a simplistic way—that is, forming an estimate of the ability of a patient to live in one of a number of different environments—in practice, assessment is a much more complex term. The systematic assessment of the physical, mental, psychological and social competence of an individual involves physicians, therapists, psychologists, social workers and, possibly, nurses. It includes an assessment of the environment in which the patient is living and of other environments in which he may live. It can be agreed, therefore, that the assessment process may require a period of attendance at the day hospital before a satisfactory plan can be drawn up.

Perhaps it might be reasonably concluded that assessment, as a reason for day hospital attendance, overlaps to some extent with rehabilitation. If the two are added together as causes for referral, they account for 73 per cent of patients referred.

Maintenance treatment

Maintenance treatment, ranked by geriatricians as the second most important function of the geriatric day hospital, follows rehabilitation. It aims to prevent any loss in the degree of independence which has been achieved as a result of rehabilitation. Specific treatment for this purpose is not always necessary. Many patients, once restored to reasonable independence, will be able to keep themselves at that level. Part of the art of geriatric medicine is to pick out patients who require maintenance treatment and who, without it, would tend to deteriorate. The definition of the point at which rehabilitation ceases and the decision as to whether or not maintenance treatment is required is one of the important functions of the regular case conference reviews of the progress of day hospital patients. The decision should be noted in the patient's case record and the various professionals should be aware of the change.

Our studies indicated that maintenance treatment was the reason for referral of 11 per cent of patients and that at any one time 20 per cent of patients were receiving it, compared with 42 per cent in the 1970 survey.[12]

Social reasons

Five per cent of patients were referred for social reasons. Of those attending the day hospital, 16.5 per cent were thought to be attending for social reasons: 13 per cent for the patient's own benefit and 3.5 per cent for that of the relatives. This may be compared with 26 per cent in the 1970 survey.[12]

This objective of day hospital care overlaps with that of other forms of day care, and the interpretation of the most suitable place for offering day care to patients on this basis is likely to vary a good deal from one area to another. A clear policy should be developed from discussion between the geriatric physicians and social workers in any area. One forum for this discussion is the health care planning team for the elderly. If the services offered by both the NHS and the social services in any area are to be effective, division of responsibility must be clearly understood by all concerned. We found that some catchment areas have no social day centre. We have also shown that the average waiting time for transferring patients to a day centre whose day hospital treatment is complete, is about six weeks. This is associated with the waiting list for the day centre which, in turn, is caused more by lack of transport than by lack of places in the day centre. Many day hospitals will retain patients while they are waiting their turn for admission to the social day centre.

Only 4 per cent of the patients taken in by the day hospital were regarded at the time to be suitable for a social day centre. But 50 per cent of patients attending day hospitals went out elsewhere on days when they were not attending–26 per cent of them to a day centre or day club!

Social day care has a very definite role, however; 37 per cent of the patients live alone.

Medical and nursing procedures

Geriatricians ranked nursing procedures as third in importance, and medical procedures as fifth. Eight per cent of the patients were referred for either medical or nursing procedures, and at any one time 13 per cent were attending for medical procedures and 6 per cent for nursing. This total of 19 per cent compares with 5 per cent in the 1970 survey.[12] But we must consider to what extent the procedures are most suited for carrying out by the day hospital, by an outpatient department or by the district nurse in the patient's own home. The main medical procedures were ear syringing and proctoscopy; others mentioned were electrocardiography and venepuncture. We find it difficult to see any reasons for patients attending day hospitals only for these procedures, unless the day hospital is also serving as an outpatients' consultative clinic. Medical procedures occupied only 7 per cent of the time which the medical staff spent in the day hospital. Nursing procedures, said to occupy 16 per cent of the nurses' time, included bathing (the most common procedure), measurement of blood pressure, surgical dressings and the treatment of ulcers.

Although not mentioned by our respondents, one might imagine that important contributions to medical and nursing care in the day hospital would include the supervision of patients with parkinsonism who are being put on to a regime of levodopa (Sinemet), the observation of the causes and frequency of incontinence, and of falls. Perhaps some of these have been thought of as part of assessment.

The stated objectives of day hospital attendance in relation to individual patients are not always reflected in the treatment which they receive. We found in a number of day hospitals that a 'package' of remedial therapy is given to all patients, regardless of the reasons for attendance or individual need.

Table 23 compares reasons for attendance with treatment received by patients attending for less than a three-month period. To these figures we may add that 12 per cent of the patients attending for rehabilitation had been attending for over one year, and that 27 per cent of those attending for maintenance had been attending for over three years.

Table 23 Reasons for attendance compared with treatment received (during attendance of less than three months)

	treatment received				
reasons for attendance	*occupational therapy*	*physio-therapy*	*speech therapy*	*special nursing*	*attendance less than 3 months*
rehabilitation	92	87	15	29	52
maintenance	81	79	–	15	19
relatives' relief	88	75	–	25	26
social	65	32	3	10	38

Notes: All figures are percentages. The table combines parts of Tables 16 and 17.

Views of patients and relatives

Patients and relatives did not perceive the purpose of the day hospital in the same way. Relatives emphasised the social and psychological benefits much more than the treatment received, and while the patients were more likely to see the day hospital as a treatment unit, with medical, nursing or remedial therapy as the most important reason for attendance, what they enjoyed was the companionship.

We were surprised to find from discussions with patients and relatives how little communication there seemed to be between them and the staff. The rehabilitative role of the day hospital could be enhanced by a partnership of relatives and staff, with instruction on how to carry out rehabilitative procedures when the patients are at home. If the relatives could be shown the objectives of rehabilitation for elderly patients, they might be more inclined to see the day hospital as a place for a course of treatment rather than for an indefinite period of companionship only. This idea could be introduced on a personal basis during individual consultations and in a standard letter sent to relatives at the start of treatment and perhaps developed in group meetings of relatives such as those held in Windsor Day Hospital at Falkirk.

It is worth remembering that when physicians talk of saving hospital beds by using the day hospital they are often not only referring to rehabilitation beds but also to long-stay beds. In achieving this latter the crucial factors are probably the relief offered to relatives or the maintenance of sufficient physical independence to allow the patient to continue living in the community.

Psychogeriatric patients

Separate provision was made for these patients in day hospitals in 36 per cent of the areas. The remainder included only 19 per where day hospitals accepted responsibility for them. We would agree with the view that separate day hospital accommodation is required for geriatric and psychogeriatric patients. Where separate accommodation is not available, a possible method of providing some relief to the relatives of demented old people might be for the day hospital to devote its facilities one day a week for this purpose alone.

Transport

Paradoxically, the only people who seemed to have few complaints about transport to day hospitals were the patients and their relatives. Only 15 per cent of the staff were entirely satisfied with the transport service. Most of the ambulance drivers criticised either the vehicles they had to use or the nature of the work itself.

We believe that the ideal vehicle for day hospital work should have forward-facing, chair-type seats, good visibility through the windows and easy communication between the driver and his passengers. It should be warm and should have a tail-lift.* It should be staffed by drivers who are doing only this type of work, either on a rotational basis or permanently, and should be used for the day hospital only.

We found it almost incredible that 70 per cent of the patients are still brought to the day hospital in multipurpose vehicles. The only reason for using such unsuitable vehicles would seem to be to allow them to be directed to accidents and emergencies. Two-thirds of ambulance drivers told us they were, either occasionally or quite frequently, directed to work of this type when they were scheduled to transport day hospital patients. The disorganising effect which this is bound to have on the whole work of the day hospital, the discomfort to patients and the waste of professional staff's time, can be easily imagined. If sitting-type vehicles cannot be deployed for the day hospital, the appropriate alternative would appear to be private cars or taxis. At the present time, about one-third of the day hospitals use transport additional to, or alternative to, that provided by the ambulance service.

*The value of the tail-lift has been questioned. Because drivers are experienced in lifting disabled people up and down steps and stairs, the extra lift into the vehicle is of little consequence. But the drivers interviewed were strongly in favour of tail-lifts and many felt this was the most important feature which their vehicle lacked.

We would support the appointment of an ambulance liaison officer. And we would stress that ambulance drivers' knowledge of the old people who are their patients is additional useful information for the day hospital staff. The drivers' criticisms were constructive and some of them found this type of work very satisfying.

Now that the geriatric day hospital is so firmly established as a regular part of the NHS, the time has certainly been reached when it requires its own separate and suitable transport system.

Day hospital provision

The DHSS's provision of two day hospital places for every 1000 people aged 65 and over in the population served would seem to be adequate, perhaps even generous, for present practice. It seems likely that a small proportion of patients could equally well be managed in social day centres. We found that half of them were able to go out, on the days they were not attending the day hospital, to social day centres, shops, libraries, pubs and so on. The number of patients able to go to social day centres might be even larger than estimated. The shortage of day centres and of suitable transport have a constraining effect.

In considering the future provision of day hospitals, or any other form of statutory provision for old people, it must be borne in mind that by the year 2006 there will be an overall increase of 62000 people aged 65 and over in the general population of Great Britain, and an increase of 645000 of those aged 75 and over. These apparently incompatible figures arise from the fact that the population aged 65–74 will have decreased by 12 per cent and the 75 and over will have increased by 23 per cent by that time. We have shown that 53 per cent of the patients now attending day hospitals are aged 76 and over.

Staffing

Just over half the day hospitals had more than one consultant and 18 per cent had three or more. In these circumstances, it is important for one consultant to have administrative responsibility while his colleagues maintain clinical responsibility for their patients. Regular consultant sessions to review patients' progress are associated with a higher degree of activity in the day hospital. It would seem, however, that where junior staff or clinical assistants provide day-to-day medical care, the consultant sessions do not in general need to be more than once a week.

The day-to-day management may reasonably be a cooperative effort with the nurse, physiotherapist and occupational therapist heading their own departments, but the nurse-in-charge appears to be the person in the best position to coordinate the smooth running of the hospital.

Our figures show that recruitment of nurses for day hospital work appears to be satisfactory—a striking contrast to the recruitment of nurses to some other parts of the hospital service, including geriatric inpatient departments. The ratio of different grades of nurses is about three trained to two untrained: 33 per cent SRNs, 27 per cent SENs and 40 per cent nursing auxiliaries. This gave a ratio of one nurse to nine day hospital places (with the average number of places at 31). We may compare this with the recommendations of the BMA working party in 1976 of one nurse to six places.[10] But if we analyse the figures in relation to the numbers of patients attended by nurses each day, we get a ratio of one to five.

The average figures for remedial therapy staff in post were one whole-time equivalent occupational therapist, physiotherapist and physiotherapy aide to an average daily attendance of 23 patients. In a 30-place day hospital this represents 42 sessions a week or 4.2 whole-time equivalents of remedial therapists and aides, exactly half the figure recommended by the BMA working party, but slightly more than the figures in Brocklehurst's 1970 survey of 49.2 sessions per week for an average day hospital of 37 places, or 40 sessions a week for a 30-place day hospital.

It is perhaps surprising that the proportion of therapists' time spent on home visits was as low as one per cent for physiotherapists and three per cent for occupational therapists. In many areas, home assessment is carried out by occupational therapists on the staff of the social services department (sometimes called a rehabilitation officer). Our interviews indicated a good rapport between these two groups. Although the proportion of time spent on home assessment is extremely small, 67 per cent of occupational therapists and 13 per cent of physiotherapists said that they undertook home visits from time to time.

Four of the 30 day hospitals had access to domiciliary physiotherapy. In one case, the physiotherapist was a full-time member of the day hospital staff, an extremely satisfactory arrangement for providing exercises and instruction of relatives at an early stage in disability—particularly in stroke illness. A close relationship between the domiciliary physiotherapist and the day hospital physiotherapist eases the patient's transition between the two departments, the more so if the consultant geriatrician has been involved in the initial referral and maintains close contact with the therapists.

Between 25 and 30 per cent of all day hospitals had no regular social worker. In some the social worker attached to the geriatric department or to the hospital provided an ad hoc service. We found, however, that if a day hospital had a social worker on the staff the weekly 'input' was considerable: on average, seven patients would be seen with an additional six hours of work on behalf of day hospital patients.

Good liaison between the hospital's geriatric department and the local authority's social services department is essential to produce a clear understanding about responsibility for individual patients, both during and after their day hospital attendance. In one-fifth of the day hospitals visited this liaison was formalised with regular meetings. In two-thirds of the day hospitals, liaison was informal, but appeared to be satisfactory.

Relationship of the day hospital to other services

The case for using the day hospital also as the rehabilitation centre for geriatric inpatients seems overwhelming. This was happening in almost three-quarters of the geriatric day hospitals of Britain. It is economical in staff and facilities and allows the easier transition from the inpatient to outpatient status—one of the most vulnerable times in the life of an elderly person, as Skeet has shown.[70]

This dual usage of the day hospital has important implications for its siting. It may seem surprising that only one-third of day hospitals were situated in the district general hospital. However, half were situated in purely geriatric hospitals, and though the concept of a hospital being used for geriatric patients alone would now seem to be outdated, no doubt most of these geriatric hospitals were involved in rehabilitation.

The day hospital may also function as the outpatient consultative clinic for the geriatric department, though only 10 of the 30 hospitals we visited did so. This function would seem appropriate only in day hospitals with immediate access to x-ray and cardiographic departments, otherwise unnecessary travelling may be imposed upon the elderly patient. The facts that the day hospital staff are particularly sympathetic to the old and the environment is geared to their need, may be advantages. On the other hand, so many elderly people attend any general hospital outpatient department that it would seem important to instil similar qualities in these departments if they do not already exist; outpatients coming for consultation do not usually require to spend the whole day in the process. There may, however, be advantages for patients discharged from the day hospital to come back to the same place for their review.

Referrals

We found it to be the exception for patients to attend a geriatric day hospital without having been seen by a physician on the staff of the geriatric department. Patients were referred by general practitioners, by other hospital consultants and, occasionally, by social workers. They were then almost invariably seen either by the consultant geriatrician or a member of his medical staff, at home, in the outpatient department, in the day hospital or in the ward. It is important, at this point in referral, that the geriatrician who sees the patient provides adequate information and guidance to the day hospital staff. A referral form is useful. It should contain the basic data, particularly about mobility, continence and drug treatment. It should outline the aims of treatment in the day hospital and the number of times that the referring physician suggests the patient should attend. From this information the day hospital staff should be able to arrange an appropriate programme of treatment. We found that this often occurred with the involvement of the physician in day-to-day charge of the day hospital.

The patients' treatment timetables need careful programming in day hospitals of any size, especially in the larger ones which may combine inpatients and day patients. The uniform 'package' of treatment offered by some day hospitals for all comers seems to be most inappropriate.

Case conferences

The multidisciplinary case conference seems firmly established as the best method of review of day hospital patients. We were surprised to find, however, that in 70 per cent of the day hospitals, case conferences were held without any active participation by the patient.

At the case conference, diagnosis should be reviewed, together with the result of any medical investigations undertaken, drug therapy and progress towards independence. The expected plan of action should be revised as necessary. In all of this the patients' and relatives' views are important and any problems arising out of the social environment need to be taken into account. Decisions about liaison with the general practitioner and community services must be made and responsibility delegated. If the general practitioner can attend that part of a case conference when important decisions about his patient are being discussed, so much the better, but for good practical reasons this is not often possible. The reason for the patient's attendance should be confirmed or redefined. At some stage during this process the patient ought to take part in the discussion. No decisions will have any effect unless the patient is in agreement.

Structure of the patient's day

The patient's day should be individually planned and usually oriented to the treatment required. Decisions about whether or not there should be a regular round for the administration of medicines have to be taken locally. Our findings were that the formal medicine round was unusual. But patients on complex regimes require to be clearly identified, and special arrangements made to assist them in taking their medication.

Most patients we interviewed felt that they had enough to do; and few complained of boredom. Generous rest periods would, therefore, seem to be important and, while there should be adequate opportunity for diversional activities in addition to active treatment, there should also be time for quiet contemplation.

Appendix
Main features of 30 day hospitals

Day hospital	District/Area	Construction	Remarks
In London			
St Matthew's	Tower Hamlets	hall built on to hospital	combined day hospital and day centre with facilities for inpatients
St Michael's	Enfield	purpose-built	in grounds of geriatric hospital
St Pancras	South Camden	purpose-built	also consultative out-patient clinic
South Western	St Thomas'	purpose-built	combined day hospital, day centre and consultative outpatient clinic
Whittington	Islington	adapted	on first floor of district general hospital
In other cities			
Bolton General	Bolton	purpose-built	in grounds of district general hospital
Burton House	South Manchester	purpose-built	part of geriatric department of district general hospital

Dudley Road	West Birmingham	purpose-built	on ground floor of new geriatric block in district general hospital
Ladywell	Salford	purpose-built	on to hospital for geriatric patients and younger disabled
Newsham	Liverpool	adapted	extension of old hospital chapel
Peterborough	Peterborough	adapted	first floor ward in geriatric wing of district general hospital
St David's	South Glamorgan	purpose-built	with rehabilitation extension in grounds of geriatric hospital
St James's	Leeds	adapted	from geriatric ward in district general hospital
Sherwood	North Nottingham	purpose-built	in grounds of district general hospital and geriatric hospital complex
Victoria Infirmary	South-eastern Glasgow	purpose-built	on ground floor of geriatric hospital, with outpatient department
Warrington	Warrington	purpose-built	on to geriatric wing of district general hospital
In small towns			
Airedale	Airedale	adapted	small room next to remedial therapy department in district general hospital (purpose-built day hospital to be developed)

Bexhill	Hastings	purpose-built	for day patients and inpatients
Biggart	South Ayrshire	adapted	small room next to remedial therapy department in geriatric hospital
Christchurch	Dorset	adapted	built on to wing of district general hospital
Guisborough	South Tees	adapted	in geriatric hospital, with small extension
Maesgwyn	Ogwr	purpose-built	in grounds of geriatric hospital
St Margaret's	Durham	adapted	basement of geriatric hospital
West Park	Macclesfield	adapted	small extension to remedial therapy department in geriatric hospital
Windsor	Falkirk	adapted	old building in grounds of geriatric hospital
In rural areas			
Hinchingbrooke	Cambridge	purpose-built	ground floor of purpose-built geriatric hospital
Lamellion	Plymouth	adapted	ward in geriatric hospital
Lluesty	Clwyd North	adapted	old hospital chapel in geriatric hospital
Pine Heath	Norwich	adapted	building in small geriatric hospital
Torridge	North Devon	adapted	with extension, remedial therapy department in geriatric hospital

References

1 ABRAMS, M. *Beyond three-score and ten: a first report on a survey of the elderly.* Mitcham, Age Concern, 1978. pp. 63.

2 ANDERSON, D.C. *Report on leisure and day care facilities for the old.* Mitcham, Age Concern England, 1972. pp. 37.

3 ANDREWS, J. *and others. A geriatric day ward in an English hospital. Journal of the American Geriatrics Society,* vol. 18, no. 5. May, 1970. pp. 378–386.

4 ARIE, T. *Day care in geriatric psychiatry. Gerontologia Clinica,* vol. 17, no. 1. 1975. pp. 31–39.

5 ARONSON, R. *The role of an occupational therapist in a geriatric day hospital setting–Maimonides Day Hospital. American Journal of Occupational Therapy,* vol. 30, no. 5. May/June, 1976. pp. 290–292.

6 BAGNALL, M.K. *Day care and social needs. Gerontologia Clinica,* vol. 16, no. 5–6, 1974. pp. 253–257.

7 BAKER, A.A. *and* CLUNN, T. *How they turned a church hall into a day hospital. Modern Geriatrics,* vol. 6, no. 12. December, 1976, pp. 16–18.

8 BEER, T.C. *and others. Can I have an ambulance, doctor? British Medical Journal,* vol. 1, no. 5901. 9 February, 1974. pp. 226–228.

9 BLAKE, D.H. *A day hospital for geriatric patients: the first twelve months. Medical Journal of Australia,* vol. 2, no. 18. 2 November, 1968. pp. 802–804.

10 BRITISH MEDICAL ASSOCIATION. BOARD OF SCIENCE AND EDUCATION. *Report of the working party on services for the elderly.* London, B.M.A., 1976. pp. 56.

11 BROCKLEHURST, J.C. *Role of day hospital care. British Medical Journal,* vol. 4, no. 5886. 27 October, 1973. pp. 223–225.

12 BROCKLEHURST, J.C. *The geriatric day hospital.* London, King Edward's Hospital Fund for London, 1970. pp. 100.

13 BROCKLEHURST, J.C. *The work of a geriatric day hospital. Gerontologia Clinica,* vol. 6, no. 3. 1964. pp. 151–166.

14 BROCKLEHURST, J.C. *and* SHERGOLD, M. *Old people leaving hospital. Gerontologia Clinica,* vol. 11, 1969. pp. 115–126.

15 COHEN, C. *Club activities in a geriatric unit. Gerontologia Clinica,* vol. 7, no. 5. 1965. pp. 281–285.

16 COSIN, L. *Architectural and functional planning for a geriatric day hospital. International Journal of Social Psychiatry,* vol. 17. no. 2. 1971. pp. 133–140.

17 COSIN, L. *The place of the day hospital in the geriatric unit. Practitioner,* vol. 172, no. 1031. May 1954. pp. 552–559.

18 *Day services: an action plan for training. Report of the working party on training for employment in day centres providing care, education and educational opportunities.* London, Central Council for Education and Training in Social Work, 1975. pp. 88. *CCETSW Paper 12.*

19 DINSE, D. *and others. Geriatrische Tagesklinik. Zeitschrift für Gerontologie,* vol. 8. 1975. pp. 451–466.

20 DOHERTY, N.J.G. *and* HICKS, B.C. *The use of cost-effectiveness analysis in geriatric day care. Gerontologist,* vol. 15, no. 5, Part 1. October, 1975. pp. 412–417.

21 DROLLER, H. *A geriatric outpatient department. The Lancet,* vol. 2, no. 7049. 4 October, 1958. pp. 739–741.

22 EASTMAN, M. *Medical noose that strangles the social work function. Health and Social Service Journal,* vol. 87, no. 4551. 29 July, 1977. pp. 1108–1109.

23 EASTMAN, M. *Whatever happened to casework with the elderly? Age Concern Today,* no. 18. Summer, 1976. pp. 9–12.

24 ELLIS, L.J. *Designing day hospitals. Gerontologia Clinica,* vol. 16, no. 5–6. 1974. pp. 294–299.

25 FAIRCLOUGH, F. *Community and day hospital care. Nursing Mirror,* vol. 143, no. 6. 5 August, 1976. pp. 67–68.

26 FARNDALE, J. *The day hospital movement in Great Britain.* Oxford, Pergamon Press, 1961. pp. xvii 430.

27 FINE, W. *Integration of a day hospital into a geriatric service. Gerontologia Clinica,* vol. 6, no. 3. 1964. pp. 129–142.

28 GLASS, S.C. *Workshops for the elderly. Gerontologia Clinica,* vol. 16, no. 5–6. 1974. pp. 285–288.

29 *Going home? The care of elderly patients after discharge from hospital. Report on the continuing care project.* Liverpool, Age Concern Liverpool, 1975. pp. v 74.

30 GOLDSTONE, H. *Planning a day hospital. Gerontologia Clinica,* vol. 16, no. 5–6. 1974. pp. 289–293.

31 GREAT BRITAIN. DEPARTMENT OF HEALTH AND SOCIAL SECURITY. *Hospital geriatric services.* London, D.H.S.S., 1971. *DS 329/71. Appendix B. Geriatric day hospitals.*

32 GREAT BRITAIN. SCOTTISH HOSPITAL ADVISORY SERVICE. *Psychiatric and geriatric day care: conference held on April 27, 1973.* Edinburgh, Scottish Hospital Advisory Service, 1973. pp. 53.

33 GREENFIELD, P.R. *A departmental view. Gerontologia Clinica,* vol. 16, no. 5–6. 1974. pp. 307–314.

34 GUSTAFSON, E. *Day care for the elderly. Gerontologist,* vol. 14, no. 1. February, 1974. pp. 46–49.

35 HAGVALL, K. *and* SUURKALA, J. *Geriatric day hospital care—experiences from a three-year study.* Lakartidningen, vol. 72. 1975. pp. 1091–1094.

36 HALL, M.R.P. *Day care and society. Gerontologia Clinica,* vol. 16, no. 5–6. 1974. pp. 300–306.

37 HIGGINS, J. *Occupational therapy in the social services. Gerontologia Clinica,* vol. 16, no. 5–6. 1974. pp. 281–284.

38 HILDICK-SMITH, M. *A typical journey to and from the day hospital. Gerontologia Clinica,* vol. 16. no. 5–6. 1974. pp. 263–269.

39 HOWAT, J.G.M. *and* KONTNY, E.L. *What price the ambulance? A survey of psychiatric day patient transport. British Medical Journal,* vol. 2, no. 6097. 12 November, 1977. pp. 1298–1299.

40 IRVINE, R.E. *Physiotherapy and the geriatric day hospital. Physiotherapy,* vol. 55, no. 9. September, 1969. pp. 352–357.

41 KAIM-CAUDLE, Prof. P.R. *The Sunderland mobile day centre.* Durham, University of Durham, Department of Sociology and Social Administration, 1977. pp. 55.

42 KENNEDY, R. *The day hospital as a rehabilitation resource in the United States. Rehabilitation,* no. 92. Jan–March, 1975. pp. 44–50.

43 KIERNAT, J. *Geriatric day hospitals: a golden opportunity for therapists. American Journal of Occupational Therapy,* vol. 30, no. 5. May/June, 1976. pp. 285–289.

44 KOFF, T.H. *Rationale for services: day care, allied care and co-ordination. Gerontologist,* vol. 14, no. 1. February, 1974. pp. 26–29.

45 KOSTICK, A. *Levindale day-care program. Gerontologist,* vol. 14, no. 1. February, 1974. pp. 31–32.

46 LITMAN, T.J. *Influence of age on physical rehabilitation. Geriatrics,* vol. 19, no. 3. March, 1964. pp. 202–207.

47 LLOYD, G. *The role of the general practitioner in the geriatric day hospital. Modern Geriatrics,* vol. 3, no. 2. February, 1973. pp. 96–101.

48 LÖBL, G. *Tagesversorgung für langzeitkranke in Skandinavien. Zietschrift für Gerontologie,* vol. 10. 1977. pp. 235–243.

49 LODGE, B. *and* PARKER, F. *Environmental modification in day care. Social Work Today,* vol. 8, no. 24. 22 March, 1977. pp. 14–15.

50 LORENZE, E.J. *and others. The day hospital: an alternative to institutional care. Journal of the American Geriatrics Society,* vol. 22, no. 7. July, 1974. pp. 316–320.

51 McCOMB, S.G. *and* POWELL-DAVID, J.D. *A geriatric day hospital. Gerontologia Clinica,* vol. 3, no. 3. 1961. pp. 146–151.

52 MARSTON, P.D. *Day hospitals: a physiotherapist's view. Physiotherapy,* vol. 62, no. 5. May, 1976. pp. 151–152.

53 MARTIN, A. *and* MILLARD, P.H. *Effect of size on the function of three day hospitals: the case for the small unit. Journal of the American Geriatrics Society,* vol. 24, no. 11. November, 1976. pp. 506–510.

54 MATTHEWS, J.C. *The social services view. Gerontologia Clinica,* vol 16, no. 5–6. 1974. pp. 318–323.

55 MEHTA, N.H. *and* MACK, C.M. *Day care services: an alternative to institutional care. Journal of the American Geriatrics Society,* vol. 23, no. 6. June, 1975. pp. 280–283.

56 MORLEY, D. *Day care and leisure provision for the elderly.* Mitcham, Age Concern, 1974. pp. 32.

57 NORMAN, A.J. *compiler. Provision of transport to outpatient departments and day hospitals: problems and possibilities. A conference report.* London, National Corporation for the Care of Old People, 1978. pp. 29.

58 OPIT, L.J. *Domiciliary care for the elderly sick—economy or neglect? British Medical Journal,* vol. 1, no. 6052. 1 January, 1977. pp. 30–33.

59 PATHY, M.S. *Day hospitals for geriatric patients. The Lancet,* vol. 2, no. 7619. 6 September, 1969. pp. 533–535.

60 PEACH, H. *and* PATHY, M.S. *Evaluation of patients' assessment of day hospital care. British Journal of Preventive and Social Medicine,* vol. 31, no. 3. September, 1977. pp. 209–210.

61 PORTER, K.R.D. *A regional view. Gerontologia Clinica,* vol. 16, no. 5–6. 1974. pp. 315–317.

62 RANSOME, H.E. *Physiotherapy in the geriatric day hospital. Gerontologia Clinica,* vol. 16, no. 5–6. 1974. pp. 274–280.

63 RATHBONE-McCUAN, E. *and* LEVENSON, J. *Impact of socialization therapy in a geriatric day-care setting. Gerontologist,* vol. 15, no. 4. August, 1975. pp. 338–342.

64 ROBINS, E.G. *Report on day hospitals in Israel and Great Britain.* National Center for Health Services Research. Department of Health, Education and Welfare, Washington DC, 1975.

65 ROBINSON, E. *Bridgnorth day centre—a case of modest success. Age Concern Today,* no. 22. Summer, 1977. p. 11.

66 ROSS, D.N. *Geriatric day hospitals—counting the cost compared with other methods of support. Age and Ageing,* vol. 5. 3 August, 1976. pp. 171–175.

67 SAUNDERS, B.M. *Nurse's role in day care. Gerontologia Clinica,* vol. 16, no. 5–6. 1974. pp. 248–252.

68 SHAW, P. *and* McMILLAN, D. *Nuffield House—a day centre for the psychiatric elderly. Gerontologia Clinica,* vol. 3, no. 3. 1961. pp. 133–145.

69 SILVER, C.P. *A jointly sponsored geriatric social club and day hospital. Gerontologia Clinica,* vol. 12, no. 4. 1970. pp. 235–240.

70 SKEET, M. *'Home from hospital': the results of a survey conducted among recently discharged hospital patients.* London, Dan Mason Nursing Research Committee of the National Florence Nightingale Memorial Committee, 1970. pp. 91.

71 STROUTHIDIS, T.M. *Medical requirements of the day hospital. Gerontologia Clinica,* vol. 16, no. 5–6. 1974. pp. 241–247.

72 SYMONDS, P.C. *Social services and day care. Gerontologia Clinica,* vol. 16, no. 5–6. 1974. pp. 270–273.

73 THOMAS, J.H. *and* WILLIAMS, M. *Geriatric day hospital. British Hospital Journal and Social Service Review,* vol. 76, no. 3978. 15 July, 1966. pp. 1323–1327.

74 THOMPSON, M.K. *A general practitioner looks at day care. Gerontologia Clinica,* vol. 16, no. 5–6. 1974. pp. 258–262.

75 TURBOW, S.R. *Geriatric group day care and its effect on independent living. Gerontologist,* vol. 15, no. 6. December, 1975. pp. 508–510.

76 WADSWORTH, M.E.J. *and others. A geriatric day hospital and its system of care. Social Science and Medicine,* vol. 6, no. 4. August, 1972. pp. 507–525.

77 WASHBURN, S. *and* VANNICELLI, M. *A controlled comparison of psychiatric day treatment and in-patient hospitalisation. Journal of Consulting and Clinical Psychology,* vol. 44, no. 4. August, 1976. pp. 665–675.

78 WEILER, P.G. *and* KIM, P. *Health care for elderly Americans: evaluation of an adult day health care model. Medical Care,* vol. 14, no. 8. August, 1976. pp. 700–708.

79 WEISSERT, W.G. *Two models of geriatric day care: findings from a comparative study. Gerontologist,* vol. 16, no. 5. October, 1976. pp. 420–427.

80 WOODFORD-WILLIAMS, E. *and* ALVAREZ, A.S. *Four years experience of a day hospital in geriatric practice. Gerontologia Clinica,* vol. 7, no. 2/3. 1965. pp. 96–106.

81 WOODFORD-WILLIAMS, E. *and others. The day hospital in the community care of the elderly. Gerontologia Clinica,* vol. 4, no. 3. 1962. pp. 241–256.

Index

References to individual hospitals will be found under the name of the town or city in which they are situated.